Crisis
Management

How to develop a powerful program
- *Build a great team,*
- *Secure executive support*
- *Be prepared for whatever happens*

Regina Phelps

Chandi Media

www.ChandiMedia.com

260 Whitney Street
San Francisco, CA 94131

415-533-1712

Crisis
Management

Published by:
> Chandi Media
> 260 Whitney Street
> San Francisco, CA 94131
> 415-533-1712
> www.ChandiMedia.com
> Info@ChandiMedia.com

ISBN: 978-0-9831143-5-2
LCCN: 2018909246

Table of contents

	Dedication	vii
	Acknowledgements and thanks	ix
	Introduction	xi
SECTION ONE: Embark on a journey		1
1	Leadership in Times of Crisis	3
2	Let's step back a moment - What is Crisis Management?	21
3	Five steps to getting a handle on soft incidents	33
4	Ten lessons in Crisis Management	41
SECTION TWO The "Five Ws and an H" of Crisis Management		51
5	Who is on the team(s)?	53
6	What does your Crisis Management structure look like?	67
7	When to activate	89
8	Where do you convene?	113
9	Why an effective crisis management program is important	129

10	How to create a top-notch Crisis Management Team and program	147

SECTION THREE Crisis process	163

11	What is Situational Awareness and why do you need it	165

12	Incident Action Plans – Roadmaps for success	183
13	Department Operations Centers (DOC) – You just might need these	195

14	Crisis Management plans	209
15	Sustained operations and your Emergency Operations Center	231

SECTION FOUR Program reassessment and reflection	249

16	Continual improvement – Crisis Management Team and program development	251

	Glossary	267

Dedication

This book is dedicated to my husband, Dave Kieffer, whose loving support and generous heart make all things possible.

Acknowledgements and thanks

First of all, I greatly appreciate my clients around the world. Together, we sort out the constantly changing threat environment and continuously pioneer new strategies and responses. Those experiences certainly informed this book.

Thanks also to my colleagues Kelly Williams who always has wise observations about our clients' challenges and Larry Yant and Meg Keehan, who edited the text.

Finally, I thank my husband, Dave Kieffer, a long-time management consultant, who read the book draft and offered some helpful thoughts.

Introduction

❝ *One thing is sure.*
We have to do something.
We have to do the best we know how
at the moment...If it doesn't turn out right,
we can modify it as we go along. **❞**

— **Franklin D. Roosevelt**
32nd President of the United States

The famous lines are from FDR's inauguration speech – *"The Only Thing We Have to Fear is Fear Itself"*. The country was in the midst of the Great Depression and people were out of work and out of hope. Even the rich and famous were suffering, so one can only imagine the plight of the common man.

Crisis management in most organizations is really a good news, bad news story. The good news is that most companies don't activate their crisis management program, team or plan very often. The bad news is that most companies don't activate their crisis management program, team or plan very often. What that means is that most organizations have never had to expend the time and energy to really figure out exactly what they need. It is most commonly done to check a box or comply with an audit finding or, worse, in the heat of a *real* crisis.

This book is based on my work since 1982 and what I have seen over and over again in companies of all sizes, all over the world. Many company leaders have not really thought about:

- Who should be on the team
- Exactly what they do (roles and responsibilities)
- How issues are brought to the surface and are assessed
- How the plan is activated
- What are the executives' roles and how do they work with everyone else
- How the team works together at the time of crisis
- Who communicates to whom and how is it done
- And so on...

For many years, I have taught a two-day exercise design class at the Disaster Recovery Journal (DRJ) conferences. We often focus on doing exercises for Executive or Corporate Crisis Management Teams. This would lead to many more questions about those teams – how they are organized, what are their roles and responsibility, how the teams would be activated, who communicates with who and so on. We would spend hours discussing these issues rather than actually doing exercise design. There is a clear need to know more.

Why now? I have never seen the worldwide threat level as severe as it is today. The chances for any company to activate its crisis management plan are much higher than ever before. Here are four top threats that could affect you:

- **Cyber Threat.** The cyber threat worldwide is extremely serious. The chance of any company getting breached – regardless of how good its information security team is – has never been greater. And the attacks are more devastating and have a much longer impact.
- **Climate change.** Climate change is increasingly causing havoc worldwide: Hurricanes, flooding, tornadoes, wildfires, heat waves and severe winter storms are more numerous and more disruptive.
- **Violence.** Every day in the United States, there is at least one mass shooting (when four people or more are killed). No part of our society is untouched: workplaces, schools, places of worship, government and military facilities have all been hit by violence.
- **Global instability.** There is a great turmoil in governments around the world – from the Americas to Africa, the Middle East, and the Philippines. Terrorist attacks kill people and disrupt international trade. Wholly-domestic U.S. companies may think they are immune, but we mustn't forget about the 9/11 disasters, which directly affected 520 businesses in the World Trade Center (and many more in the adjacent area).

I have designed crisis management teams, both strategic (executive) and tactical (general management), in companies on four continents. I have done speeches and workshops and written articles on this topic but decided that more was necessary. This is a cookbook, if you will, on the development of crisis management teams. The goal of this book is to tell you everything you need to know to build a successful crisis management program. I hope I succeed.

This is iterative work...your program, plan and team will get better over time. After each activation, after each exercise. The goal is to keep moving your team forward.

Please contact me with your questions and let me know about your progress.

ONE

Embark on a journey

> ❝ *To embark on the journey towards your goals and dreams requires bravery.*
> *To remain on that path requires courage.*
> *The bridge that merges the two is commitment.* ❞

— **Steve Maraboli**
Speaker, author and
behavioral scientist

We are about to embark on a journey together into the land of crisis. No, no - don't run away yet, there is nothing to fear. Our traveling together will not require a passport, special shots, or a tolerance for spiders or reptiles. This journey will take you into a deeper understanding of what makes a leader and a team successful when dealing with a crisis and learn where leaders and teams have failed in the past.

The good news is that there is a lot you can do to bring process and order into the middle of a crisis; that's what this book is all about. This overview section digs into some basic issues related to crisis management:

- Skills that leaders and teams need to be successful.
- A glossary to make sure we are all speaking the same language.
- Lessons from the past that we can all learn from and hopefully not do ourselves.
- The difference between a hard and a soft incident and how to track down where a soft incident may come from in your organization.

CHAPTER 1

Leadership in Times of Crisis

Chapter topics
- *Essential preparation*
- *Three scenarios*
- *Required leadership skills*

66 *It takes 20 years to build a reputation
and five minutes to ruin it.
If you think about that,
you'll do things differently.* 99

— **Warren Buffet**
Founder, Berkshire Hathaway.

Introduction

Serious preparation is required to successfully manage in a crisis. Being prepared requires two things from each and every responder:

1. Be in a **constant state of readiness**. Since you won't know the *precise nature* of the crisis in advance (timing, location, or specifics required at the time), people who may be

managing a crisis must always be in a *constant* state of readiness, as near to instantaneous as possible. Think in terms of "instant-on."

2.   Have a **wide range of contingencies** at your disposal so you will be prepared for many possibilities. And in some cases, despite prior training, plans, experience, and exercises, what you have and what you do may still not be enough.

Planning for the "Worst Case"?

One of the things I often hear continuity and emergency professionals say is that they plan for the "worst-case scenario." Whenever I hear that, I immediately stop them. This is simply not true. Continuity professionals don't plan for the worst-case scenario. They plan for what they think will happen, what is called a "routine" emergency. What they plan for may be a really bad situation, but there really is not enough time, money, or risk appetite to plan for the truly worst-case scenario.

Different types of crises

"Routine" Emergency

To be clear, *routine emergency*[1] does not mean easy. A routine emergency can still be difficult and challenging. In this context,

---

[1]   Howitt, Arnold & Leonard, Herman, Managing Crisis: Responses to Large-Scale Emergencies, CQ Press, February 11, 2009, page 5.

routine refers to the relative predictability of the situation that permits advanced preparation. This kind of risk is in the company's risk profile, and the company likely has been able to take advantage of lessons learned from prior experiences. Continuity professionals probably have thought about what to plan for and what is needed, and they have typically trained and done exercises for those situations. Crisis/Incident management, crisis communications, business continuity, and disaster recovery plans are filled with strategies to manage routine emergencies. It is, after all, what continuity professionals do for a living.

"Crisis" Emergency

A *crisis emergency*[2] is a much different animal. These types of events are distinguished by significant elements of **novelty**. This novelty makes the problem much more difficult to diagnose and then deal with. This type of emergency can have the following characteristics:

- The threats have never been encountered before and, therefore, there are no plans to manage it. Think of September 11, 2001, and those planes hitting the World Trade Center and the Pentagon. No one had imagined something like that could be a possibility. The United States was genuinely not prepared for a disaster of that magnitude.
- It may be a familiar event, but it is occurring at unprecedented speed. Developing an appropriate response to this

---

2   Ibid, page 6.

type of situation is extremely challenging. Superstorm Sandy (2012) was such an event. The storm moved up the Eastern Seaboard with most of the hurricane models predicting it would go out to sea. The European hurricane models forecast that it would bear west and hit New Jersey and New York head-on. Even though it made landfall as "just" a tropical storm, it devastated the region, and is just behind Hurricane Katrina as the most expensive hurricane in U.S. history.

- There may be a confluence of forces, which, while not new individually, in combination pose unique challenges to the response. New Orleans had prepared for a hurricane, and it also prepared for a levee failure – just not both at the same time. When Hurricane Katrina hit and the levees subsequently failed, it was a crisis like this country had never seen. As of 2018, it remains the most expensive hurricane in U.S. history.

The novel nature of a crisis emergency becomes a game-changer. Plans, processes, training, and exercises that may work well in routine emergency situations are frequently grossly inadequate in a crisis emergency and may even be counterproductive. You quickly realize that you have to start from scratch. In other words, you have to improvise.

The crisis emergency also requires different capabilities. The plans and behaviors used for routine emergencies just won't work. The first thing that must be done is to *identify* the elements of the novelty-determine what makes this situation so different from others.

In a cyber attack or breach, this novelty is often surprising. You might begin the process thinking it is one thing, and then over time, realize it turned out to be something quite different. For example, you may think you are dealing with a routine IT problem or outage. Over time, you may see it is something far more significant and sinister.

Once you identify the real problem and understand that the routine plans won't work, you have to improvise response measures that will be suitable to cope with the unanticipated aspects of the incident. You're in new territory because this hasn't been done before. Created out of necessity, these responses may be actions quite different than any taken before. Handling a crisis emergency may feel like you're building an airplane while flying it at the same time. It's not pretty and it makes people uncomfortable but you may not have any other choice.

Lastly, in a crisis emergency, you must respond in creative ways and, *at the same time*, be extremely adaptable executing these new and improvised solutions. You have to be on "full alert" at all times, as you don't know if or how the situation will change, and you must be prepared to shift at a moment's notice. All of this makes people quite anxious. (During an exercise, this anxiety often manifests itself in varying degrees of excessively loud voices or hushed voices, frantic activities, and nervous laughter.)

An emergent crisis[3] is a different animal. It poses special challenges in terms of recognizing its novelty early on because it

---

3   Ibid,page 6

may look a lot like a "routine" emergency in its early stages. Only later does it reveal its unusual characteristics. Part of this problem is that leaders may be slow to see the new features. They keep telling themselves that they know what they are seeing, thinking "I know how to manage that," "I know about hurricanes," or "I know how to handle an earthquake." The leaders then fail to see the differences. They become wed to their original solution, so they are slow to discover that what is needed is really something quite different.

A great example of an emergent crisis was the SARS (Severe Acute Respiratory Syndrome) infectious disease outbreak in Toronto. This was a classic emergent crisis. The disease first appeared in the Guangdong province in China in November of 2002. The first Canadian index case occurred in late February 2003 after a woman visited Hong Kong. She died in Toronto in early March 2003 of unrecognized SARS because no one imagined she could have it. Subsequently, the transmission chain from the Canadian index case resulted in at least six generations of transmission, four of which were contracted while at a hospital. The Toronto SARS outbreak occurred in two waves; the first was from March to April 2003, the second was from April to July. In total, 44 people in Canada died from SARS, approximately 400 became ill, and 25,000 Toronto residents were placed in quarantine.[4]

A second example of an emergent crisis is a cyber breach or

---

4   SARS Outbreak in Canada, Canadian Environmental Health Atlas, http://www. ehatlas.ca/sars-severe-acute-respiratory-syndrome/case-study/sars-outbreak-canada

challenging malware infection. The IT department may tackle it as a routine glitch. They believe they know what it is. As they continue to work, unbeknown to them, it begins to morph and change. They blithely believe they know what it is, and think they have it under control. It is only after time has passed, and the situation gets worse, that they realize it isn't what they thought.

Seven essential actions required to manage a crisis

In managing any of the three crises, leaders need to push through

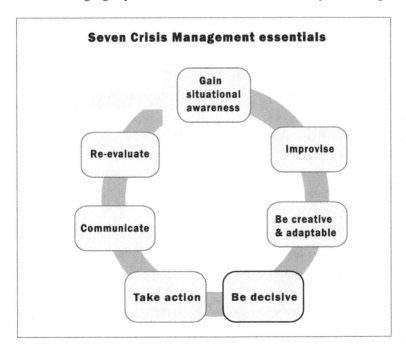

Seven Crisis Management essentials

Gain situational awareness

Improvise

Be creative & adaptable

Be decisive

Take action

Communicate

Re-evaluate

a series of action steps (and they must have the skills to do it):

.1. Gain and maintain situational awareness
2. Improvise
3. Be creative and adaptable
4. Be decisive
5. Take action
6. Communicate
7. Re-evaluate

Gain situational awareness

Situational awareness is perhaps one of the most critical skills needed in a crisis. It is the ability to identify, process, and comprehend the critical elements of information about what is happening to you and your organization in relation to the crisis. Put more simply, it's *knowing what is going on around you...* even as it may be changing.

Before an incident occurs, you need to carefully decide how to perform these five critical actions in the heat of battle:

1. **Who?** Determine who will gather information.
2. **Collect.** Amass the information and keep updating.
3. **Validate.** Confirm the information.
4. **Process.** Digest the information.
5. **Disperse**: Display and communicate that information to the key players.

It is essential to work out these actions in advance, and then practice and refine them in an exercise. Of course, these steps need to be continually refreshed throughout the event.

Who is responsible for collecting and updating the information? It could be one person, but it is likely a group. During an event, gather and validate the key facts of the incident. This is often under conditions of great chaos and uncertainty. Information may be confusing or conflict with other sources. You need to obtain situational awareness from multiple sources. Some of those sources might be:

- Media, both traditional and social
- Emergency responders
- Employees and contractors
- Vendors
- Customers
- City, county or state governments
- Government agencies

Once you have the information, validate it by seeking corroborating evidence. Sometimes this means you have to triangulate numerous sources in order to be sure what you've learned is true. In some cases, though, you may not be able to confirm the data. In that case, be sure to note it as "not confirmed."

In addition to obtaining the information, decision-makers must take in the data and process its real meaning. They must "project forward" the implications of the information they now know and then anticipate possible consequences of a fast-changing and still-shifting incident. That means, as part of this skill, they must generate possible alternative courses of action and assess which solutions hold the most promise of dealing with the current conditions.

Lastly, the information needs to be dispersed. Display it in the command center, in virtual tools, and in incident action plans and reports. This information will be used to develop the talking points used to communicate the situation.

Improvise

In a crisis, leaders often examine newly-updated information and review their routine plans and checklists, then find that their response is not adequate. They then realize that customization is required. The presence of significant novelty calls into question whether routine plans will work. This means that the situation may require unplanned and unrehearsed actions in order to move ahead.

In a true crisis, leaders, often under extreme pressure and with high stakes and compressed timelines, must formulate a new approach to the situation. They must execute new responses or a combination of responses to manage the crisis. In other words, leaders must improvise.

This may cause a certain amount of angst in some leaders who are more comfortable with the familiar. Leaders need to be careful that they are not holding onto an old and comfortable response that is not working. Instead, they may need to move forward quickly to embrace a new and untested solution.

Be creative and adaptable

A crisis requires approaching new problems with new thinking and creative and adaptable responses. Leaders must find ways to see and appreciate the novel elements in a crisis and understand that a different approach may be required. While this may be difficult for some to do in the heat of battle, hopefully, they will have practiced this in periodic exercises. Training leaders through simulations can allow them to practice this critical skill in a safer environment.

Some of the ways to foster creativity and adaptability include:

- Focus attention on what is new about this particular situation. People are drawn to the familiar. Don't just think about what is the same?" Instead ask, "What about this is different?"

- Ensure that diverse viewpoints are heard. Have a mixed team with a variety of backgrounds and experiences. Homogenous teams may not deliver the best results. The younger, newer or eccentric person in your team who has "different" ideas might have the perfect solution to solve the crisis. That, of course, assumes people will listen to him/her.

- Systematically require additional thought. Determine if the set of possibilities is large enough at the beginning and decide how to look for one or more better alternatives. Consider having a team of trusted advisors who can look over the leader's shoulder and question decisions and plans. This is sometimes called the "Team B" approach. "Team B" is a separate team of highly skilled individuals watching the primary team's plan from multiple angles. They act as a secondary planning team, but without the pressures of the crisis. Team B can often spot issues or options that "Team A" overlooked.[5]

A leader and his/her team must adapt rapidly to a fast-changing crisis. By its nature, a crisis changes quickly, and the first response will likely not be the final response. A critical thing to remember is that in a crisis situation, the leader cannot be wedded to a single strategy. They must continue to take in new information, listen carefully, and consult with frontline experts who know what's happening. In other words, don't fall in love with your own solutions and ideas.

Be decisive

It's the moment of truth. Someone must make a decision. Everyone knows a leader who struggles to make decisions. The inability to make a decision is a disaster within the disaster.

- Once situational awareness has been reviewed, *AND*
- The response has been improvised, *AND*
- Creativity and adaptability have been exercised *THEN*
- The leader must *make a decision*

If, after a period of time, it becomes apparent the wrong decision was made, make another one. The role of the leader is to keep the team and the organization moving forward. Put one foot in front of the other and keep moving.

Sometimes leaders are reluctant to make a decision because they don't have complete information. Unfortunately, it is a rare situation when all of the information is available during the

---

5   Mitchell, Gordon R., "Team B Intelligence Coups", Quarterly Journal of Speech Vol. 92, No. 2, May 2006, pp. 144-173.

incident. Most of the information may not even be available until the incident is long over. Not having "all" the information can cause some leaders to freeze. At this point, the leader needs to take a deep breath, review what s/he does know, and make a decision. Not making a decision is not safe. It is a passive form not doing anything. It solves nothing and makes things worse.

When things are happening quickly, no one person can have actual control of the situation, but a leader can assume control. In other words, *the disaster can't be controlled, but the response to it can be.* The leader's job is to assume the mantle of leadership and, well, lead!

Communicate

I don't think I have ever heard anyone say in a major crisis, "My company communicated too often with me," or "I always felt like I knew what was going on." It is highly doubtful that would ever happen. Indeed, what is needed in any crisis is clear, crisp, concise, and timely communication. This is absolutely essential.

Set realistic expectations for communication ***in advance*** — perhaps in the employee handbook, e.g., here's what you can typically expect if there's an emergency or challenging event in our buildings [plants, facilities, etc.] And then communicate early and often as events unfold. Of course, the intent isn't to alarm people, but don't be afraid to speak to the magnitude of the situation. People need to hear what is going on, even if the news is not good. And with the prevalence of social media sites, your people (or their family members or friends) will start Tweeting or posting Facebook messages that may be exaggerated or wholly false. It may take hours or days for you to set the record straight. In a worst case scenario, the bad information could live on for weeks, months or years. (Remember the passenger dragged off United Airlines plane — captured on iPhones.?)

The way to head this off is for you to get on those main social media as quickly as possible and provide timely and reliable information. Otherwise, your people will be getting half-baked accounts which may be unnecessarily scary while getting increasingly frustrated about your "radio-silence."

When reviewing your company's crisis communications plan, be sure it includes the following information:

- Who are critical audiences?
- What tools are used to communicate?
- Who communicates with whom (i.e., who owns the relationship)?
- What is the initial message? (Since it's likely no one will know what the exact event is, the initial message can be something like, "{An event} has happened, we are actively investigating and will report shortly.")

Putting the above information into a communications matrix will produce several key pieces of information:

- *Who* needs to be communicated with?
- *Tools* that will be used?
- *Who does* that communicating?
- *What* will be said in the first message?

These are very powerful tools to have at your fingertips.

Take action

This is the second moment of truth: Act! Make the decision, and then do it. At this point, it's time to enact the plans and observe the response.

One critical aspect of taking action is to ensure that there are sufficient feedback loops to assess response to the new plan and adjust accordingly. Keep checking in and determine how the plans are doing. At the same time, don't forget to take in new situational awareness information, and adjust accordingly.

Biases and other challenges

A word of warning: Be aware of the dangers of biases, preconceived notions and simple bad judgements. Personal biases are always present, but they can be a serious issue at time of crisis. Here are examples of biases that tend to appear in crisis situations :

- **"Know-It-All."** Overweighing one's experience. It sounds like, "Been there, done that." When you hear someone in the command center say, "I know about hurricanes," be worried.
- **Illusion of experience**. A tendency for individuals to think that they have more experience than they actually do, and to attempt to convince others that they do, too.
- **Overconfidence**. In one's abilities and in one's ability to predict the future. It's the (faulty) belief that they can control the future.
- **Failure to observe** or believe disconfirming evidence.

The leader doesn't believe what is happening right before her or his eyes.

- **Escalation of commitment**. Once it's noticed that a decision is not working, people double-down and recommit to the solution rather than rethink it.
- **Bandwagon effect**. The tendency to do or believe things because many other people do or believe the same. "The more the merrier!"

We have all seen people who express these biases in the midst of a crisis. Perhaps we even see those traits in ourselves from time to time. If people start saying things like…"Don't worry, I've been in lots of earthquakes and I know how to manage one," start worrying and keep your eye on them!

Re-evaluate

Lastly, be prepared to do regular assessments at set intervals to re-evaluate and reassess progress. This provides the ability to tweak (or do a major overhaul) of the plan. Ask these questions over and over:

- "How are we doing?"
- "What are we missing?"

This would be a good place for "Team B" to chime in.

While assessing progress, the leader should be sure to be aware of and check for cognitive bias in him/herself and the team, and measure performance against the objectives. Once this assessment is done, recommit to your plan, tweak it, or redesign it. The key thing is to keep the team and the organization moving forward.

Summary

Review these seven essentials with the leadership and crisis management teams. Design exercises that allow them to practice these skills and build muscle memory. Remember the famous quote from Thomas Edison when asked about creativity: "If we all did the things we are capable of doing, we would literally astound ourselves." This simple statement recognizes a primary law of human creativity, namely, the great potential hidden in each of us. Work with the crisis management team now to develop these skills, so that in the next crisis, they will astound themselves..

CHAPTER 2

Let's step back for a moment – What is crisis management?

Chapter topics
- *Aligning definitions*
- *Event terminology and team structures*
- *Business Continuity and Management Framework*

❝ *The Chinese use two brush strokes
to write the word 'crisis.'
One brush stroke stands for danger;
the other for opportunity.
In a crisis, be aware of the danger—
but recognize the opportunity.* **❞**

— **John F. Kennedy**
35th President
of the United States

Introduction

When you pick up a book with the words "Crisis Management" in its title, you are likely thinking about it from your professional viewpoint. But which perspective is that? Business continuity, communications, risk management or technology practitioners will all view it through their lens. Executives may come at it from a completely different place. Before digging into this topic, I'd like to take a moment to frame the conversation for the chapters that will follow.

So, what is crisis management?

Crisis management is… well, it depends on who you ask. A quick internet search produces a plethora of responses and approaches. Here are just four of the answers to that question. Different professions use a different lens to view a crisis:

- A business continuity professional may say that a crisis is the identification of threats to an organization and its stakeholders, and the methods used by the organization to deal with these threats.[6]
- A crisis communications professional may say that a crisis is the application of strategies designed to help an organization deal with a sudden and significant negative event.[7]
- A risk manager may say that crisis management involves

---

6   Crisis Management, Investopedia, http://www.investopedia.com/terms/c/crisis-management.asp
7   Crisis management, WhatIs.com, http://whatis.techtarget.com/definition/crisis-management

assessing potential threats, finding the best ways to avoid those threats and dealing with threats before, during, and after they have occurred. Risk management is strategic- while crisis management is a response.[8]

- A technologist may say that a technological crisis arises as a result of failure in technology, which could be problems in the overall systems leading to a technological crisis, a mechanical breakdown, corrupted software, or a cyber attack or breach crisis.[9]

- An executive may say that it is a process by which an organization deals with a disruptive and unexpected event that threatens to harm the organization, its stakeholders, or the general public.[10]

Those definitions may sound similar, but when you peel them back (and take a deeper look at those sites), you will discover that they each come to the definition from a very specific angle. It might be reputation or brand management, crisis communications and social media responses, the continuation of critical business processes or technology services, or, perhaps, what executive management does in a time of crisis. Most are very singularly focused in their interest and approach and written to a specific audience.

For the purposes of this book, I prefer a more broad and com-

---

8   Flick, Steve, What Is the Difference Between Crisis and Risk Management?, bizmanualz, https://www.bizmanualz.com/solve-business-problems/what-is-the-difference-between-crisis-and-risk-management.html

9   Types of Crisis, Management Study Guide, http://www.managementstudyguide.com/types-of-crisis.htm

10   Wikipedia, Crisis Management, https://en.wikipedia.org/wiki/Crisis_management

prehensive approach to the definition, as used in *Guideline for Incident Preparedness and Operational Continuity Management (ISO 22320)[11]*, referring to "operational continuity management." It includes three definitions that get to the heart of what this book is about:

- **Operational Continuity Management:** A holistic management process that identifies potential impacts that threaten an organization and provides a framework for building resilience with the capability for an effective response that safeguards the interests of its key stakeholders, reputation, brand and value-creating activities.
- **Operational Continuity Management strategy:** An approach by an organization that will ensure its recovery and continuity in the face of a disruptive event, crisis or other major outage.
- **Operational Continuity Management program:** The ongoing management and governance process supported by top management and resourced to ensure that the necessary steps are taken to identify the impact of potential losses, maintain viable recovery strategies and plans, and ensure continuity of functions/products/services through exercises, rehearsal, testing, training, maintenance and assurance.

The goal of this book is to identify a holistic crisis manage-

---

11   ISO 22399, 3.20, 3.24, 3.21 page 4.This standard was published in 2007 and subsequently removed by ISO. It still, however, provides a holistic definition to work with. https://www.iso.org/standard/50295.html

ment framework by building a resilient strategy, process, and team that will ensure the organization's continuity and recovery in the face of a disruptive event or major crisis.

Terms and definitions

In your organization, what do you call a "situation" or "predicament"? Which is a minor occurrence and which is more severe? The words that we most commonly hear include "event," "incident," "emergency," "disaster," "crisis," and "catastrophe." Let's first begin by looking at the common definitions for those words.

To be unbiased, they are in alphabetical order.
- Catastrophe
  - A momentous tragic event ranging from extreme misfortune to utter overthrow or ruin *(merriam-webster. com)*
- Crisis:
  - A stage in a sequence of events at which the trend of all future events, especially for better or for worse, is determined; turning point *(dictionary.com)*
  - An extremely dangerous or difficult situation *(dictionary.cambridge.org)*.
  - A time when a difficult or important decision must be made *(oxforddictionaries.com)*
- Disaster:
  - A sudden calamitous event bringing great damage,

           loss, or destruction *(merriam-webster.com)*
- ○ A sudden, calamitous event that seriously disrupts the functioning of a community or society and causes human, material, and economic or environmental losses that exceed the community's or society's ability to cope using its own resources *(International Federation of Red Cross and Red Crescent Societies, IFRC.org)*
- Emergency:
  - ○ Sudden, urgent, usually unexpected occurrence or event requiring immediate action *(dictionary.com)*
  - ○ An unforeseen combination of circumstances or the resulting state that calls for immediate action *(merriam-webster.com)*
- Event:
  - ○ Something that happens *(merriam-webster.com)*
  - ○ A thing that happens or takes place, especially one of importance *(oxforddictionaries.com)*
- Incident:
  - ○ An instance of something happening; an event or occurrence *(oxforddictionaries.com)*
  - ○ An event, especially one that is either unpleasant or unusual *(dictionary.cambridge.org)*
  - ○ An unplanned interruption to an IT Service or reduction in the quality of an IT service *(ITIL 2011)*

In Chapter 7, when we discuss activation criteria and severity levels for incident assessment, we will use these terms in the order of severity:

- Incident (minor)
- Emergency (moderate)
- Crisis (severe/catastrophic)

The naming of names

To add to the confusion, the name that an organization calls their respective strategic and tactical teams who respond to an incident, emergency, or crisis can be all over the map. Here is a list of team names we've seen in our practice:

- Company Emergency Response Team
- Local Incident Response Team
- Corporate Incident Response Team
- Local Incident Management Team
- Corporate Incident Management Team
- Local Crisis Response Team
- Corporate Crisis Response Team
- Local Crisis Management Team
- Corporate Crisis Management Team
- Executive Management Team
- Executive Leadership Team
- Senior Leadership Team
- Crisis Steering Committee
- Emergency Operations Center or EOC (this one is weird because an EOC is a physical place, not a team)

For many years, we recommended that our clients use the

term "crisis management team." We noticed, however, that companies were often reluctant to call this team together because of the word "crisis." The team wasn't activated because the situation never became what they considered a "crisis." That led us to change the name to "incident management team," implying that the team could be called together for smaller incidents rather than just the big "crisis." This got further validity with ISO 22399 (which addresses incident preparedness and operational continuity) and NFPA 1600 (which specifically refers to incident management systems).

Fast-forward to the release of ISO 20000 and ITIL, which refers to "incident management" as an IT service management (ITSM) process area. Technologists had used the word "incident" for years, but now it really embraced the "incident management" term – and there was no going back. We found this to actually create more confusion about which incident management team was activated, or which incident management team was responding to the incident. So to avoid further confusion, we made the decision to go back to calling our client teams "crisis management teams."

In this book, we will work with the following four team names:

- Department Operations Centers (DOC) – The name for response departments which have a separate physical or virtual command center. These are departments that often have a "field response," commonly the Security, Facilities, and IT departments.
- Local Crisis Management Team (LCMT) – The crisis management team at a regional or lower level office.

66 Plans are of little importance,
but planning is essential. 99

— **Winston Churchil**
Prime Minister of the
United Kingdom

- Corporate Crisis Management Team (CCMT) – The crisis management team at a corporate headquarters.
- Executive Crisis Management Team (ECMT) – The senior management team tasked with performing strategic activities during a crisis.

If your company is small (fewer than 500 employees) with just one location, you will likely have a single Crisis Management Team and will not require all of the different iterations described above.

Clear as mud? Don't worry, it will clear up as we go along.

Business continuity management framework

Lastly, it is important to discuss the framework of this crisis management model and how it fits into the larger business continuity management (BCM) framework. In the field of BCM, there are four major silos:

1. Emergency response
2. Business continuity
3. Disaster/technology recovery

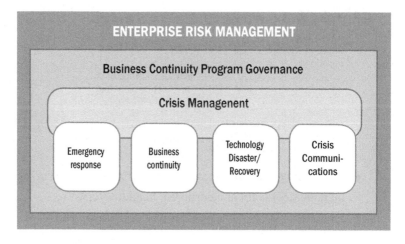

4. Crisis communications.

Without a well-defined crisis management process, strategy and team, these four activities can be four free-standing silos that are not coordinated and are being managed individually. The crisis management process is the umbrella that the four silos are housed under during a crisis.

This is how we view a business continuity management framework. It is comprised of three distinct sections:

- Crisis Management:
  - Emergency response
  - Business continuity
  - Disaster/Technology recovery
  - Crisis communications
- Business Continuity Governance.
- Enterprise Risk Management.

Surrounding the entire crisis management process is Business Continuity Program Governance, a critical – and often missing – component. Governance is about authority, decision-making, and accountability. Within any organization, the term "governance" determines who has authority, who makes the decisions, and how the organization is kept accountable. There are three benefits from including this in your program:

- Creates an internal commitment; overcomes the inertia that often prevents "overhead' programs from developing.
- Defines the end-state; establishes the size, scope, and structure of the program.
- Defines the mechanisms for maintaining the program over time; ensures that the capability, once built, remains viable.

I'll dig more into Business Continuity Program Governance in Chapter 10.

And around the entire program is Enterprise Risk Management. This diagram does not imply that a Business Continuity Management department reports up to the Enterprise Risk Management office, although in many organizations, it does. It does, however, demonstrate that effective Business Continuity Management is about mitigating and preparing for identified risks when possible, and then when required, responding and helping the organization recover.

Summary

It is important to make sure that we are all on the same page before we get too far into crisis management framework, process, strategy, and forming of teams. The goal of this chapter is to make sure that our glossaries are aligned and that we are speaking the same language. Look at the terms you use now in your organization. Do they make sense after reading this chapter? Keep this in mind as you read this book. As long as you're going to make a lot of structural changes to an existing program, you may as well start calling the pieces by more meaningful words!

CHAPTER 3

Five steps to getting a handle on soft incidents

Chapter topics
- *"Hard" incidents*
- *"Soft" incidents*
- *"Soft" incident reporting structures*

66 *If you can't describe what you are doing as a process, you don't know what you're doing.* **99**

— **W. Edwards Deming**
Renown 20th Century
management consultant

Introduction

"Soft" organizational crises have been around for decades. New and far more menacing "soft" crises have emerged in recent years – leaving many, perhaps most, organizations wholly unprepared. The first really widespread soft crisis was the great "Y2K" issue at the turn of the century. It was a walk in the park compared to what is going on now.

"Hard" versus "Soft" incidents

The types of calamities that can create a real crisis can be placed into two categories "Hard" (physical) and "Soft" (intangible).

"Hard" incident

A hard incident is one you can tangibly see and feel; in other words, an event where there is a physical impact. Fires, earthquakes, floods, tornadoes, hurricanes, mudslides, violence at work, bombs – these situations all produce a physical, tangible result, a hard incident.

Hard incidents are somewhat predictable. By that, I mean you've seen this movie before. They typically have a beginning, a middle, and some defined ending. You have an idea of what to expect. Once it is over, the recovery can begin, even if it is slow and painful. You usually know who the players are and who is in charge within your organization. Outside authorities, like police, fire, or federal or state agencies are often involved, especially in the beginning. Indeed, they may even take over during the most acute phases of the response.

Traditional company emergency response, business continuity, technology recovery, crisis communications, and crisis management plans have long been built to address this type of incident. Until quite recently, just about all programs revolved around hard incidents.

"Soft" Incident

Is a "soft" incident the opposite of a "hard" incident? Well, yes and no. Soft incidents are events where there is an impact to an organization's business and potential damage to the brand or reputation with little or no physical damage. Soft incidents are insidious – they usually don't leave behind any physical evidence. Many companies have begun to recognize increased pressure, both internally and externally, to respond to new, more untraditional incidents, what we're calling 'soft' incidents.

A list of soft incidents would include all of the following:
- Malware
- Ransomware
- Data compromise resulting in stolen customer information (e.g., Equifax, Target)
- Denial of service attacks
- Website crashes
- Inability to process orders due to a technology disruption
- Fraud
- Product recall
- Product failure
- Loss of key vendor(s)
- Employee misconduct (i.e. sexual harassment)
- Diseases (i.e., pandemic influenza, Ebola)
- Reputational disasters (i.e., Wells Fargo account fraud or United Airlines customer treatment)

Sometimes it's hard just to discover a soft incident. It often gets worse before it gets better. How do you report, assess and manage the incident? Determining who is in charge in a soft incident can be tricky for several reasons:

- Ambiguous internal reporting structures.
- Unclear who is actually in charge because so many hands are involved.
- "Murky" because it's difficult to get a handle on the incident.
- Politically challenging because few want to "own" the problem.

> **66** *Efficiency is doing things right; effectiveness is doing the right things.* **99**
>
> — **Peter Drucker**
> Renown 20th Century
> management consultant

Five steps to getting a handle on soft incidents

There are five steps to getting a handle on soft incidents:

1. Identify where soft incidents originate.
2. Map the current response process.
3. Determine if assessment teams are in place.
4. Review how incidents are currently assessed.
5. Document how the soft incident process plugs into the

current crisis management process.

STEP ONE: Identify where soft incidents originate

- Technology. Perhaps the most challenging and menacing vulnerability. Examples include malware, ransomware, Denial of Service (DoS) attacks, phishing, and spoofing.
- Communications: The challenge of keeping ahead or at least even with all the potential media stories, both traditional and social, after an incident.
- Key lines of business. Fraud, product recall, product tampering, product quality, accounting improprieties, customer service.
- Human resources: Sexual harassment, threats to employees or from employees.
- Senior management and boards of directors: Fraud, embezzlement, embarrassing statements or behaviors, sexual harassment, drug and alcohol abuse, questionable business investments or associations, misuse of company funds or physical assets like cars or planes.

STEP TWO: Map the current response process

Explore the issues identified in Step One and map how a typical incident would unfold. Literally plot it out on a whiteboard. Start from when the incident occurs. Document what happens next. Identify who is involved and how it progresses. Those steps alone may lead you to discover places where an incident may go unrecognized for an extended period of time or existing assessment teams you hadn't heard of before.

STEP THREE: Determine if assessment teams are in place

In an effort to manage these types of incidents, departments often set up their own assessment teams to deal with outages or issues. Your first challenge is to identify these departments. Some are very formal and established; others pop up as the need arises. Look in these departments and see if you have such teams in place:

- Technology:
  - ○ Incident Management Team
  - ○ Security Incident Response Team
  - ○ Privacy Response Team
- Communications:
  - ○ Traditional and social media response teams
- Key lines of business:
  - ○ Fraud Team
  - ○ Product Recall Team
  - ○ Customer Support or Customer Service Team
- Human Resources:
  - ○ Threat Assessment Team
- Senior management.
  - ○ Audit Team or Committee
  - ○ Risk Team or Committee
  - ○ Executive Committee
- Board of Directors:

○ Enterprise Risk Team or Committee
○ Executive Committee

STEP FOUR: Review how incidents are currently assessed

Once you find a team, group, or even one person who handles this type of incident, ask if they have procedures, protocols, or plans for handling and managing the situation. If they do, ask for the documents and review them carefully. If they don't have any written documentation, you will need to interview them to determine how an incident is handled as well as the path that it takes through their department or group. You need to know:

- When the issue arises, what happens first?
- Who calls whom?
- Are there any escalation criteria?
- When do others outside the department get engaged?

This will often require you to speak to a variety of individuals to get the entire story. Pull the right people into the room to get the whole picture. If possible, ask for previous examples of issues that have occurred and how they were handled. In particular, ask how they were escalated and to whom they were referred.

STEP FIVE: Document how the soft incident process plugs into the current crisis management process

This last step is crucial. You need to know how a soft incident gets plugged into the existing crisis management process. This is where many issues seem to go unattended within a depart-

> ❝ *There are no secrets to success.*
> *It is the result of preparation, hard work,*
> *and learning from failure.* ❞
>
> — **Colin Powell**
> Retired four-star general, U.S. Army

ment and only emerge when the situation is a true crisis.There should be some written criteria that provides some quantitative or qualitative information for the initial team to use in deciding if or when to escalate. This is discussed at length in Chapter 7.

Summary

Soft incidents are emerging as a significant threat to organizations of all sizes and shapes. In particular, the cyber threat is focusing executive management and Boards of Directors on the topic of crisis management in an unprecedented and urgent manner. Spending time now to walk through the five steps of getting a handle on soft threats at your organization is essential.

CHAPTER 4

Ten lessons in Crisis Management

Chapter topics
- *Ten common crises lessons*
- *Avoid similar mistakes in the future*
- *Communication remains a major stumbling block*

❝ *Those who cannot remember the past are condemned to repeat it.* **❞**
— **George Santayana**
Poet and novelist

Introduction

Before we dig deep into how to create a great crisis management team, let's take a moment to look back on what we call "crisis lessons." In our years of practice, we have seen many different companies all over the world make the same mistakes time and time again. Reflection is one of the key skills and habits of a great leader. When you reflect on past experiences, you can learn from the mistakes, get ideas on different ways to approach a problem, and, with that, gain a new perspective. The goal of this chapter is for you to explore ten common crisis lessons and then ask yourself if any of these are present in your organization today.

Crisis lessons

As you read through the crisis lessons ask yourself: are these issues present in my organization right now? Where? How do they manifest? Have they gotten in our way before? If so, what happened? Make notes as you reflect on each one of these lessons and document the areas that may need additional examination as you develop your program.

1. Declare the disaster and activate as early as possible.
2. Staff initially to a high-enough level.
3. Issue clear and consistent instructions to employees.
4. Delegate authority to those who have been tasked.
5. Assume and plan for some degradation in team members, plans, and/or systems over time. In other words, closely monitor effectiveness.
6. Avoid two common syndromes:
   a. "Been there, done that!"
   b. "We're a really smart group, and we'll figure it out when it happens."
7. Make decisions; keep moving forward.
8. Reassess and readjust when necessary.

9. Keep aware of what is going on i.e. maintain situational awareness.
10. Communicate, communicate, communicate. And never forget about social media, and the power of an individual to affect your company.

Declare the crisis and activate as early as possible

Many organizations are reluctant to declare a crisis. The emerging issue might be inside a department which keeps working on it, believing that it will resolve soon. You've heard that plea: "Just give me five more minutes!" It might be that the group (technology, engineering, facilities, finance, security, etc.) trying to solve the problem is reluctant to ask for help, or they don't want to escalate it due to fears that they might be perceived or judged by others as "incompetent." Whatever the reason, the longer an organization waits, the more damage can be done. People need to know that there is nothing wrong with escalating the situation and activating your team so the problem can be assessed. If after a few hours you realize that it isn't as big of a crisis as once imagined, you can stand down the effort and look at the experience as a great training opportunity.

Staff initially to a high-enough level

When a crisis occurs, it is often not clear how many people you need to manage it or what skills might be required. In the beginning of a crisis, companies often send everyone home and then realize that key skills are missing, such as expertise in a particular business subject matter or strong administrative support. Look at your team staffing and carefully assess what you might need. Some of the areas that are most commonly overlooked are administrative support and additional individuals to monitor and track traditional and social media. You don't want too many people, but conversely, you don't want too few.

Issue clear and consistent instructons to staff

Companies are often slow to communicate to staff in a crisis. Perhaps executives think they don't know enough to say anything, so they aren't sure what to tell staff to do. At a minimum, you need to tell them what you know. This may be as basic as "We are aware that there is an issue, we have assembled a team, we are investigating the situation, and we'll get back to you with more information as soon as possible." If you fail to communicate, they will find out themselves, whether through the informal grapevine at work or the global grapevine – Twitter and FaceBook – and will decide for themselves what to do. Use all available tools to communicate with your employees. Hopefully this will include the use of an emergency notification system.

Delegate authority to those who have been tasked

During a crisis, when you give someone the responsibility to complete a task, also give them the authority to do so. Many times assignments may be given out, but they are given with caveats as well, something along the lines of "Before you execute or complete the task, come back and tell me what is going on so I can approve it." If you give someone a task to do, give them the authority to complete it as well. Don't hamstring your team in a time of crisis. One of the solutions to this problem is for executives to actively participate and/or approve the selection of the key leaders of the crisis team so they are comfortable with the person and confident in their knowledge.

Assume and plan for some degradation in team members, plans, and/or systems over time

Most companies don't plan for an incident to last more than a few hours, perhaps a day. When you read a business continuity or crisis communications plan, there is little guidance for a longer activation. Staffing is often thin and recovery procedures are not thought out too far in advance. This means the team will likely wear out and exhibit signs of fatigue, poor decision-making skills, and the plans – and people – will run out of steam. You need to know this will happen and have plans in your back pocket to augment staffing and recovery plans.

Avoid two common syndromes

There are two syndromes that I have seen over and over that make me both laugh and cry: "Been there, done that!" and "We're a really smart group, and we'll figure it out when it happens.""

Been there, done that!"

This is a great example of cognitive bias that was discussed in Chapter One. Individuals create their own "subjective social reality" from their perception of the situation. For example, I personally have experienced many earthquakes, so I could consider myself an "earthquake expert" and therefore know all that I need to know about earthquakes. That bias may mean that I don't really see what is happening in this current earthquake because I think I know it all. When I hear people expressing the "been there, done that" mindset, I am always concerned that they will not see what is directly in front of them and will make assumptions. Assumptions are dangerous in managing any crisis – never assume anything. Be clear about what is a fact and what is an assumption and act accordingly.

"We're a really smart group, and we'll figure it out when it happens."

This is one of my all-time favorites. I have heard this from leaders who tell me that they have no need for a formal crisis management process or team because after all, "We're a really smart group and we'll figure it out when it happens." The group may, indeed, be a "really smart group," but I am here to tell you: I don't care how smart you are, I don't care how bright you and the group are. When the Bad Thing happens, you need clear roles, responsibilities, processes and strategies that have been developed and tested in advance. You can't make those things up in the middle of a crisis. There are many who have failed trying.

Make decisions – Move forward

Great leaders must be decisive. They must know how to make

decisions as it pertains not only to their survival but also to the success of their organizations. In day-to-day business, leaders want complete information before making a decision. In a crisis, "complete information" is often not available, or conflicting. In a crisis, leaders often have to make decisions with incomplete information because that is all they have. If you make a decision and then later find out it was a mistake, make another. The leader's job at time of crisis is to keep moving the team and the organization forward.

Reassess and readjust when necessary

So, you've made a decision, and the team and the plans are moving forward. How do you know if you have to adjust? What is your feedback loop? Is there a way to get feedback on the impact of the decisions and actions being taken by the team so they can evaluate performance and then either power on or change? This feedback is critical. One of the best ways to get it is through the incident action planning process (Chapter 12) where assessments are conducted on a regularly scheduled basis, and objectives and plans are adjusted accordingly based on updated information. If you don't have this as part of your crisis management process, you could be at risk for missing subtle changes or knowing whether cognitive bias may have snuck into your assessments.

Keep aware of what's going on, maintain situational awareness

Situational awareness is simply knowing what is going on

❝ *We spend a great deal of time studying history, which, let's face it, is mostly the history of stupidity.* ❞

— **Stephen Hawking**
Theoretical physicist, cosmologist, author

around you. It sounds simple but isn't always easy. On a personal level, being aware of what is going around you on a daily basis allows you to make better decisions. In a crisis, knowing what's going on is essential and can literally mean the difference between life and death. For an organization at time of crisis, how information gets to the crisis team is critical. Where it comes from, how to validate and assess it, and how to organize it and provide it so that the crisis management team can make good decisions will be addressed at length in Chapter 11.

Communicate, communicate, communicate

Organizations are often very slow to communicate at times of crisis. This creates a communications vacuum and as Aristotle once postulated, "horror vacui" ("nature abhors a vacuum"). This means that others will rush to fill in information, which is problematic on many levels. And never (never, ever, never) forget about social media, and the power of a single individual on the internet to create great misinformation and turmoil (or worse). What often slows the release of communications is the approval process.

Summary

Take a serious look at the ten crisis lessons and look back at the last five years of incidents at your company (near misses and full-on events). Now ask yourself: what can I learn from these? Have we done the appropriate planning, preparation, mitigation and training to prevent these things from occurring in the future or managing them more effectively if they do happen?

The "Five Ws and an H"
of Crisis Management

*66Someone is sitting in the shade today
because someone planted a tree
a long time ago. 99*

— **Warren Buffet**
Founder, Berkshire Hathaway

When trying to really understand a topic, it can be helpful to use a "tried and true" methodology. For that reason, I thought the "the five Ws and an H" would be the perfect tool. These are basic questions to ask when information gathering or problem solving. They are used in journalism, police work, research, and other areas across many disciplines. The "five Ws and an H" is a simple formula for getting the complete story on a topic. I have taken a bit of liberty and modified the questions a bit to cover everything you need to know to build a great crisis management team:

- Who?
- What?
- When?
- Where?

- Why?
- How?

By using this simple and yet inclusive approach, the aim is to give you what it takes to build a well-crafted crisis management program. When you dig deeply into these questions, as we will do in the next six chapters, you will get a good grasp on what you need to have in place to check all the boxes of a great program.

Here is where we are going:

WHO is on the team(s)/ *Chapter 5*

WHAT your operational structure looks like/ *Chapter 6*

WHEN to activate/ *Chapter 7*

WHERE to convene/ *Chapter 8*

WHY this is important/ *Chapter 9*

HOW to create a top-notch crisis management program/ *Chapter 10*

Who is on the team(s)?

Chapter topics

- *A "helicopter view" to design a program*
- *Using a tier system for each location*
- *Building out your crisis teams*

❝ *We do not learn from experience, we learn from reflecting on experience.* **❞**

— **John Dewey**
Philosopher, Psychologist

Introduction

The goal of a Crisis Management Team is to protect an organization (people, business, and reputation/brand) from the adverse effects of a crisis by providing an effective response to the incident. A well-structured and practiced team can truly make the difference during the incident's critical "Golden Hour" and beyond.

The "Golden Hour" term was first described by R. Adams Cowley, MD, at the University of Maryland Medical Center based on his personal experiences and observations in post-World War II Europe, and then in Baltimore in the 1960s. Dr. Cowley recognized that the sooner trauma patients reached definitive care – particularly if they arrived within 60 minutes of being injured – the better their chances of survival.[12] It may sound like an odd comparison, but take a second look. What your company does in those first few minutes and hour(s) makes all the difference in the world. To do that, the first thing you need is a sound structure in which all the players know their roles.

Mapping your world

"Mothership"

We first begin this work by focusing on what I call the "mothership"[13] or the corporate headquarters. If you first figure out the process at this level, the rest of the structure will flow from there. Since this chapter discusses who should be on the team, we will start first at the top of the organization and then work down from there.

---

12   Eisele, Charlie, "The Golden Hour", JEMS, August 31, 2008 http://www.jems.com/ articles/2008/08/golden-hour.html

13   A large spacecraft or ship from which smaller craft are launched or maintained. Oxford Dictionary https://en.oxforddictionaries.com/definition/us/mother_ship

Helicopter view

Let's begin by taking a helicopter view of the holdings. By that, I mean we need a broad sweeping view of the overall organization to see what we must deal with before we can plot out the right structure. We start at the mothership and then expand the view if there are other locations. There are three issues to discuss here:

- Size: The overall size of the organization.
- Locations: The number of company locations.
- Culture: The unique culture of the organization that may influence this structural logic.

Size

For smaller organizations (approximately fewer than a thousand employees), you will likely only have one crisis management team that is responsible for both strategic and tactical response activities. This may cause the senior team to wear multiple hats; alternatively, they may bring in others to support more of the tactical roles.

Larger organizations should have two crisis management teams. One team would be comprised of senior executives respon-

sible for strategic activities, and the second one would be a tactical team made up of operational managers who will manage the response and recovery activities

Map your response network and teams

Maps can be remarkable tools for understanding the world and how it works, and how everything is interconnected. Once you are clear about the size of the corporate team, you can begin to frame your larger response network and the key people you need on your team(s).

Get the people in the room who understand your entire organization so you can get the map right. You can do this "mapping exercise" as a whiteboard activity. Get a large conference room with a big whiteboard or flipcharts (and, of course, associated supplies like different colored markers, post-it notes, and erasers).

Start at the top by drawing the appropriate boxes for the corporate teams as you see above. Then look at what is below that level. Do you have other locations, such as regional offices, manufacturing facilities, supply/distribution facilities, warehouses, or sales offices? Note all of those. Are there other facilities that report up to them? If so, note them as well. Keep drawing and building it out.

Now stand back and look at your "map." Do you have all locations accounted for? Add, subtract, and modify as you need to in order to have it all laid out in front of you. Make sure the reporting structures are clearly noted.

For organizations with several locations, the schematic will likely look something like this:

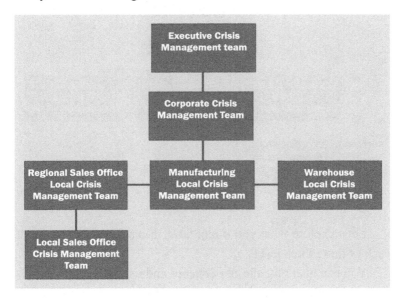

Designate a tier level

Now that you can clearly see the world in front of you, let's dig a bit deeper. If you have multiple locations, developing a clear road map about what each location should have in place for crisis management (and other things) is extremely helpful. This is most commonly done by breaking them into "like groups" or tiers.

There is a logical separation at the different levels of the teams noted above that might look something like this:

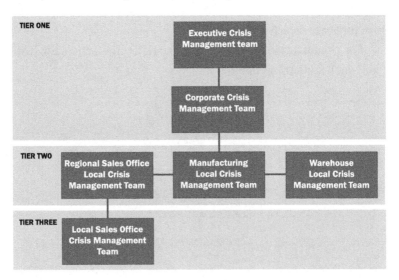

Let's explore what you might have in place and/or require at each of these three levels.

You can also take the tier concept and use it for other activities within the Business Continuity Management umbrella, e.g your emergency response program. Here you would note what Emergency Response Team), and training (CPR, First Aid, AED)

Tier	Team	Crisis management requirement
1	**Executive Crisis Management Team (ECMT)**	**ECMT Team**
1		Plan
1		Annual exercise (solo)
1		Annual exercise with CCMT
1	**Corporate Crisis Management Team (CCMT)**	**CCMT team**
1		Incident Assessment Team
1		Plan (full plan)
1		Annual exercise with ECMT
1 & 2		Annual exercise with a Tier 2 location
2	**Local Crisis Management Team (LCMT)**	**LCMT team**
2		Local Incident Assessment Team
2		Plan (abbreviated as appropriate)
2		Annual exercise (with or without CCMT)
3	**Crisis Management Team (CMT)**	**CMT team (could be just a few people)**
3		Plan (checklist)
3		Annual exercise (focus on communication and reporting protocols)

are required at each tier level. This makes it easy for someone to see the requirements and activities you have at each location for audit purposes and for reviews with your business continuity steering committee and senior management.

Culture

One other challenge in organizing your crisis management program is your company culture. Some executives don't want to let go of the management of a crisis at any level of the organization. This makes dealing with the response activities more difficult. Indeed, in a larger organization, it can render others below those individuals ineffective in their roles. It needs to be addressed as it comes into play in some organizations.

It may be a "CLM" (career-limiting move) for you to tell your executives that they shouldn't be managing everything in a crisis. Perhaps you can point to other organizations that utilize a different crisis management structure from yours as noted above. Or bring in a third party who might be able to demonstrate the inefficiencies. Another great way to demonstrate faulty thinking is to do an exercise and make it big enough that you can demonstrate the kind of "system overload" that can occur with a very small group of people trying to manage a major crisis.

Building out the teams

Now that we can see the entire landscape, let's build the teams.

Executive Crisis Management Team (ECMT)

The ECMT is comprised of the senior executives, what is often called the "C-Suite," as in CEO, COO, CIO, CFO etc. This team often has between five and nine members. If your organization is on the smaller side (less than a thousand employees), the ECMT will likely perform the functions detailed in this and the Corporate

Crisis Management Team description (below); in other words, it will do both strategic and tactical functions.

Executive Crisis Management Team roles and responsibilities

This team has big responsibilities but a short job checklist. The ECMT role at the time of crisis is to:

Make strategic policy decisions.

Make strategic financial decisions.

Act as senior relationship manager for key corporate relationships such as employees and their families, government officials, regulatory bodies and strategically important stakeholders.

Act as media spokesperson as deemed appropriate and recommended by the Communications executive.

While there are only four things on the list, the responsibilities of those four things are extensive. The types of decisions the ECMT makes will have a major impact on the entire organization, as well as guide the recovery activities of the tactical teams – not to mention the reputation of the company both internally and externally.

Executive Liaison position

In order for the ECMT to get information from the Corporate Crisis Management Team (CCMT, see below), a useful strategy is to have a designated senior individual act as liaison between the two. The individual in charge of the CCMT often has too much to do to be successful at keeping the ECMT apprised and managing the CCMT as well. A liaison position is critical as it provides a bridge between the two teams and helps to make sure that communication is flowing back and forth, and that decisions and issues are communicated promptly.

Corporate Crisis Management Team (CCMT)

The CCMT is the tactical team of operational managers who will lead the response and recovery activities for the organization. These individuals are responsible for all the recovery activities and for implementing ECMT decisions. This team activates to support the recovery of the corporate headquarters, but it also could activate to support the recovery of other company locations.

Examine your company organizational chart and the departments that should be on this team will jump out at you. The list very commonly includes:

- Business Continuity
- Communications (including all of the communicators such as Public Relations, Public Affairs, Government Affairs, etc.)
- Compliance
- Enterprise Risk
- Facilities
- Human Resources
- Insurance
- Key lines of business
- Legal
- Insurance
- Meeting and Travel
- Payroll
- Purchasing
- Safety
- Security
- Technology

Corporate Crisis Management Team roles and responsibilities

Each of the departments on the CCMT should have their own checklist that details their primary roles and responsibilities on the team. These checklists should be included in the Crisis Management Plan (see Chapter 14) and reviewed and used whenever there is an exercise or an activation.

Local Crisis Management Team (LCMT)

The LCMT is the tactical team of operational managers who will lead the response and recovery activities at the local level. These individuals are responsible for all the recovery activities and implementing the CCMT decisions.

The members of this team will be those who are local to the site. The list very commonly includes:

- Facilities
- Human Resources
- Key lines of business
- Safety
- Security
- Technology

It may also include others, dictated by which key departments are working at that location.

Local Crisis Management Team roles and responsibilities

Each of the departments on the LCMT should have their own checklist that details their primary roles and responsibilities on the team. These checklists should be included in the Crisis Management Plan (see Chapter 14) and reviewed and used whenever there is an exercise or an activation.

Crisis Management Team (CMT)

This team is likely very small with just a few individuals participating. For example, if it is a local sales office, it would be the office leader, her or his administrative person, and perhaps another individual or two with key local responsibilities.

Crisis Management Team role and responsibilities

This CMT's role is focused on life safety and situational awareness. This team has four key responsibilities:

- Life Safety: Making sure employees, contractors, and/or visitors are safe
- Liaison with emergency responders: Working with local emergency responders
- Damage Assessment: When possible, conducting an initial damage assessment based on the incident
- Notification: Notifying the "next level up," i.e., ensuring that those individuals know about the incident and can provide the appropriate response

Summary

To understand the entire crisis management process and issues at your organization, it is essential to first begin by mapping out the company and then carefully assigning teams at all of the identified levels. In some cases, unofficial structures already exist. Take those as a baseline and work with local teams to ensure that everyone has their concerns met.

CHAPTER 6

What does your Crisis Management structure look like?

Chapter topics

- *Common structures for the tactical crisis teams*
- *The Incident Command System*
- *Characteristics of a good leader*

❝ *If you don't know where you are going you'll end up someplace else.* **❞**

— **Yogi Berra**
New York Yankees
catcher and philosopher

Introduction

You now know who needs to be on the tactical crisis management team, but how do you organize them to function at their optimum level? In this chapter, we will explore what structure makes the most sense for your organization and present two options for your consideration: "Business-as-Usual" and the Incident Command System (ICS).

Your Crisis Management structure

A crisis occurs. People know they are on the "crisis management team." They assemble and start working, trying to manage the situation. What does that team structure look like? Are they organized for maximum efficiency? Do they know who reports to whom? Does everyone know her/his specific roles? In order to manage effectively, there must be a well-defined organizational structure for the team. Absolute clarity on this issue is critical!

An organizational structure is used to define a hierarchy within the crisis team. It identifies each job or task that needs to get done, its purpose, and its reporting relationship within the team. This structure establishes how the team operates, manages, and communicates the response and recovery activities required at a time of crisis.

A structure also lays out the specific responsibilities that govern the work of the team. Responsibilities must be clearly defined. Each team member must have a job description (something as simple as a checklist will do) that defines the duties for each position. Clear reporting relationships are essential for everyone to understand their responsibilities and reporting functions.

A thoughtful crisis management structure allows for the flow of information into the team and within the team during the activation. It should be created to ensure that team members work in a coordinated fashion and that communication is built into the structure. This will also ensure that sufficient resources (both human and material) are applied to identified objectives and that deadlines are met.

"Business-as-usual" structure

The most common crisis structure is "business-as-usual." A manager is selected to be the person in charge of the crisis team. This structure is one where individuals stay within their "usual" departments. Reporting and communication relationships do not change, and the manager of that department or group will likely be the person who is the "carrier" of information back and forth from the crisis team to the department. It is a silo structure that presents a variety of communication and collaboration challenges.

"Business-as-usual" structure pluses

- No training required, it is what team members do every day
- Communication within the department is the same as during "business as usual" – so everyone in that department knows the rules

"Business-as-usual" structure minuses

- Silos
  - All activities on the crisis management team are done within a collection of discrete silos, making communication and collaboration between and among crisis teams more challenging.

- Reporting
  - Getting a good view of the overall impact of the crisis is far more difficult. The individual in charge of the crisis team must speak to many individuals to get a full report and see the whole thing.
- Conflicting or incomplete information
  - The silo structure can foster isolation and teams not having complete information. There can also be conflicting or inaccurate information, which can lead to people making assumptions that are potentially incorrect.
- Duplication of effort
  - The silo structure also more easily allows for multiple groups to be working on the same problem unaware of what others are doing – which also means that other key issues might not be getting worked on at all.
- Authority
  - Having departments in a silo structure can create a situation where people are competing overtly or covertly to be in charge.
- Resources
  - If there are limited resources, a silo structure doesn't easily allow for determination of necessary resource allocation. Each silo would have its own set of priorities, and there isn't anyone to determine priorities appropriate for the entire company.

Organizations often stick with "business-as-usual" structures at time of crisis simply because they don't activate very often. They weigh "How often do we activate?" against "How much effort would it take to have a different system of operation?" It's like a simple math problem. They don't believe that there are enough compelling reasons (i.e., activations) to require the additional effort that comes with a different structure. This type of thinking can limit the effectiveness of the response right from the get-go.

Incident Command System structure

Let's look at another option, the Incident Command System (ICS for short). My goal is to demonstrate that the ICS provides an *ideal structure* in a *business setting* for what I call the Six Cs:

1. Command
2. Control
3. Coordination
4. Collaboration
5. Communication
6. Consistency

First, what is ICS?

ICS is a well-organized, *team approach* for managing critical incidents. It is a management system designed to enable effective and efficient crisis management. It provides a standardized approach to the command, control, and coordination of a crisis by providing a common hierarchy for facilities, equipment, personnel, procedures, and communications, all operating within a common organizational structure.[13]

History of the Incident Command System

In 1970, there was a disastrous wildfire in Southern California that resulted in 16 deaths, over 700 destroyed structures, more than 500,000 acres burned, and over $234 million in damage over 13 days.[14] At the incident (field) level, there was confusion caused by the differences in terminology used, organizational structures, and operating procedures between the various response agencies. At the agency or coordination level, the mechanisms to coordinate and handle competing resource demands and to establish consistent resource priorities were also inadequate. As a result, ICS was developed by an interagency group in Southern California called FIRESCOPE.

By the 1980s, ICS was being used across the country, not only in wildfire management but in day-to-day fire operations in many cities. However, in October 1991, the now-infamous Oakland firestorm occurred. It was a large suburban wildland/urban interface conflagration. The same problems present in the 1970s reappeared in 1991 when 400 engine companies, 1500 personnel, and 250 agencies tried to work together to put out the fire.

As a result of that fire, California Senator Nicholas Petris introduced a bill establishing the Standardized Emergency Management System (SEMS). The framework of SEMS includes Incident

---

13   "Incident Command System Resources," FEMA https://www.fema.gov/incident-command-system-resources

14   "History of ICS," EMSI, http://www.emsics.com/history-of-ics/

Command System (ICS), multi-agency or inter-agency coordination, the Master Mutual Aid Agreement (MMAA) and system, and the operational area concept.[15] By 1993, SEMS and ICS were a statewide mandate in California.

Fast-forward to 9/11. Despite previous ICS successes, the same "6C" issues surfaced in New York City and Washington, D.C., following the attacks on the World Trade Towers and the Pentagon. This structural flaw was well known at the time and was addressed in the numerous reports after 9/11. This ultimately resulted in President George W. Bush signing Homeland Security Presidential Directive-5, which directed Homeland Security to develop and administer a National Incident Management System (NIMS). NIMS/SEMS provides a clear and consistent organizational structure for agencies involved in responding to emergencies.[16] ICS then became a requirement for all federal, state, county, and city agencies. It is what all of the emergency responders in your community use as well.

ICS management characteristics

ICS has eight management characteristics that make it a powerful management and organizational tool. As you read through each of these hallmark characteristics, ask yourself if your current crisis management process provides this type of structure and built-in support.

---

15   "SEMS Guidelines", California Emergency Management Agency, November 2009, pages 4 – 5, http://www.caloes.ca.gov/PlanningPreparednessSite/Documents/12%20SEMS%20Guidelines%20Complete.pdf

16   "Supplemental Information: SEMS, NIMS and ICS", CDSS, page 1, http://www.cdss.ca.gov/dis/res/13Supplemental%20NIMS%20PG.pdf

Manageable span control

Manageable span of control is defined as the number of individuals one supervisor can manage effectively. The ICS recommended span of control is between three and seven immediate subordinates, with the optimum being five. The number may vary depending on the needs of the organization and specifics of the incident.

Common terminology

A common set of terms is essential in any system. It's especially important when diverse groups are involved in the response. A common terminology among company facilities and emergency responders allows teams to work together across a wide variety of crisis management functions and situations, minimizing confusion.

Modular/scalable organization

As an incident's complexity increases, the crisis management team should be able to expand from the top down as functional responsibilities are delegated. All incidents, regardless of size or complexity, will always have an Incident Commander (IC). The crisis management team may expand or shrink according to the needs of the situation because you only activate what's needed.

Integrated communications

There needs to be an interoperable communications plan and streamlined procedures for more effective communications. This can include standard operating procedures, a common communications plan, common equipment, and common terminology.

Unified command structure

This allows departments with different functional authorities to work together effectively without affecting individual department authority, responsibility, or accountability. The team works together under a set of defined objectives and an incident action plan.

Consolidated incident action plans

Incident Action Plans (IAPs) guide response activities and provide a concise means of capturing and communicating an organization's incident priorities, objectives, strategies, and tactics in the contexts of both operational and support activities. I believe that IAPs are one of the most important aspects of ICS. Even if you decide not to use ICS, you should still incorporate the IAP process into your crisis management team.

Pre-designated command centers

Command Centers that are appropriate for the risk and hazards of the organization must be pre-designated. There should always be a primary location identified, likely within your facility. A secondary location should also be identified, one that is outside your facility, maybe a few blocks or a few miles away (this could easily be a hotel room or another company location). There may also be a tertiary location identified, if, based on your risk assessment, it is appropriate. An example of needing a tertiary location is if you are located in close proximity (fewer than 50 miles) to a nuclear power plant. Some of our clients in high-risk areas of the country (such as Washington, D.C., where there is a greater chance of nuclear or chemical attack) have three specified locations.

Comprehensive resource management

This allows the organization to maximize and ration if necessary resource use, provide accountability, reduce requests, streamline the acquisition process, and consolidate the control of single or limited resources.

Incident Command System structure PLUSES

- All of the above! The eight management characteristics of ICS pretty much nails it.
- For organizations with multiple locations, if all locations are set up the same way using the same terminology, it makes it easier to plug in another team to assist or provide support.
- All the emergency responders who come to assist you use ICS, too. You'll be "speaking their language."

Incident Command System structure MINUSES

- It's something different, therefore it requires training and exercises to make it functional. (Of course, you need to be doing training and exercises anyway, right?)
- The different reporting structure may be awkward for some people. During an activation, people will be report-

ing through a different structure than during their regular day job.

- The terminology is different than the company's usual terms.
- Senior management may not understand who reports to whom, or they may believe that this process somehow usurps their role or function.

If your current crisis management process doesn't have these management characteristics, you might want to consider adopting ICS.

ICS Team Structure

The ICS structure is comprised of five teams:

- Command
- Operations
- Logistics
- Planning
- Finance & Administration

When people want to learn about ICS, many end up at the FEMA website, which is where most of them get turned off. In government, the ICS structure has many boxes with odd titles (at least to most public company ears) like "sections," "branches," "divisions," "groups," "strike teams," and "task forces." Most private sector folks look at the organizational chart and all those boxes and teams, and think, "Nope, this is not for us."

Hang on and take a deep breath. There is tremendous value in the main ICS core team, which is actually fairly simple. This core team will be our focus.

Before I dig into the team descriptions, please note the terms in the chart below. I have used the "regular" ICS terms in bold in each box. In three team boxes I have also added a possibly more "understandable term" to use that makes sense in most organizations. We always try to get our clients to use the standard ICS terminology but if it gets in the way of them understanding the process, then we opt for more "business friendly" terms.

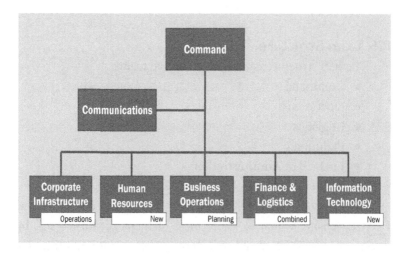

Command Team

The Command Team is comprised of the Incident Commander, Communications team (above), and some type of administrative support. In some cases, a Safety and Liaison Officer may also be included. A liaison to the Executive Crisis Management Team (if you have one) would also reside on this team.

The Command Team is responsible for:

- Setting priorities and objectives and is responsible for overall command and responsibility of the incident
- Oversees all of the team functions
- Resolving conflict in the teams
- Implementing policy decisions from Executive Management
- Providing interface to Executive Management

Incident Commander: Responsible for leading the response and recovery efforts. The leader may have a variety of different titles: Incident Commander, Emergency Operations Director or Manager, Crisis Manager, or Command Team Leader. Pick a title that works best for your company's culture.

Liaison Officer (if applicable): Responsible for coordinating with representatives from assisting agencies, such as police and fire. Sometimes this function is performed by the Facilities Department (normally residing on the Operations team).

Safety Officer (if applicable): Responsible for monitoring incident operations and advises the Incident Commander on all matters relating to the health and safety of the team during the incident. The Safety Officer has emergency authority to stop and/or prevent unsafe acts during operations. Most private sector ICS teams don't have a separate safety officer. This function is usually fulfilled by Human Resources.

Executive liaison (if applicable): If you are using a designated senior individual to act as liaison between the Executive Crisis Management Team (ECMT) and Corporate Crisis Management Team (CCMT), that individual would sit with the Command Team. This allows them to see and hear the most information, and to be present and participate in all briefings.

Administrative support: This is a critical support function in the Command Team. (The Incident Commander will often use her/his routine administrative support person for this role.) Activities include documenting the Incident Action Planning sessions, maintaining the Command Team status boards, answering phones, directing queries, and acting as an important traffic cop for the Incident Commander.

Communications: Communications reports directly to the Incident Commander. However, the team members are not likely to be seated with the Command Team. Communications can be comprised of Corporate Communications, Government Relations or Affairs, Public Relations, Social Media, Web, Marketing, Community Relations, Investor Relations, and/or any other communications functions or groups in the organization. They have three primary responsibilities:

1. Gather and verify information.
2. Develop and coordinate information.
3. Distribute information and evaluate.

This will be discussed in depth in Chapter 13.

Operations Team (Corporate Infrastructure)

In the *public sector*, the Operations team is where you will find all those departments with direct response activities such as police, fire, or department of public works. In the *private sector,* these are departments with "front line" response and recovery activities, and usually include:

- Facilities
- Security
- Technology
- Safety

These departments are the "backbone" aspects of the business, providing all the necessary requirements and support for all the other departments to function. They are responsible for all tactical operations necessary to develop and carry out the recovery plans. This normally begins with the initial damage inspections and goes all the way to restoring functionality. Their ultimate goal is to restore the business to "business as usual."

In the *private sector,* it is not uncommon for the IT team to be a separate team due to the complexity of the department and function. A technology team would include all Technology infrastructure, applications and network as well as Information Security. In this case, there would be five teams reporting up to Command instead of four.

The head of the Operations Team is often called the Team Leader or Section Chief.

Human Resources

In the *public sector,* the Logistics Team provides for all the support needs for the incident, such as ordering resources, transportation, supplies, food service, and medical services for incident personnel. In the private sector, the majority of those activities are done by a procurement department, which is firmly in the world of Finance. We initially tried to place Finance in the Logistics Team, but it never worked – they wanted to be in Finance with others from their department. So, in our *private sector* model, we created a Human Resources Team. It includes Human Resources, Employee Assistance Programs (counseling services), and supporting employees by providing food, shelter, and transportation as part of the recovery effort.

The head of the Human Resources Team is often called the Team Leader or Section Chief.

Planning (Business Operations)

The Planning Team is responsible for the collection, evaluation, and dissemination of information concerning incident development. Team members take the information that comes from Operations and the Incident Action Planning sessions, crack open their business continuity plans, and develop appropriate plans based on the incident's current status. They evaluate the current information, apply their "intelligence" (business continuity plans) to the situation, and develop a response plan for the recovery of time-sensitive business processes. The team is comprised of the key lines of business, plus the Business Continuity and Legal departments.

The head of the Planning Team is often called the Team Leader or Section Chief.

Finance, Logistics & Administration

The Finance , Logistics & Administration Team is responsible for providing the financial services functions needed by the entire team; they also are responsible for documenting incident expenditures. The team is tasked with establishing a paper trail for all incident expenditures used for reimbursement and insurance purposes. Additional activities include:

- Processing payroll
- Procure supplies and equipment
- Issuing emergency purchase orders
- Delivering cash
- Raising limits on corporate credit cards
- Working with insurance companies regarding reimbursement
- Notifying worker's compensation insurance companies

This team is comprised of members from Finance, Risk, Insurance, Payroll, Treasury Operations, and Procurement. This team often starts small but grows as the response effort continues. They are also active well after the response phase has ended, often dealing with insurance companies and agencies regarding reimbursement.

The head of the Finance, Logistics & Administration Team is often called the Team Leader or Section Chief.

ICS benefits

I hope at this point in the chapter, you can see that using the ICS structure in your crisis management team has many benefits:

- Has a clearly defined flow of information and resources within and between all ICS teams. This is particularly helpful for companies with multiple locations.
- Allows for coordination between teams.
- Allows for rapid mobilization, deployment, and tracking of resources.
- Provides a way to see the development of trends and patterns.
- Minimizes confusion and errors.
- Mimics the same system used by emergency responders.

Incident Command System – "Like"

I have some clients who say, "I like the ICS model, but my company will never go for it. It sounds too militaristic." Or, "I like the structure, but it seems too different from what we do today." I understand both of those sentiments.

To address these comments and views, try playing a game with some of the people who are in those mindsets. The goal is to group similar or like departments together that would work together in a crisis, regardless of their current reporting structure. Bring everyone into a room with a large whiteboard and lots of post-it notes. Write the name of a department on a post-it, one department per post-it.

Now, start by asking the group this two-part question: "How would your teams or departments work together to maximize communication and response efficiencies, and how would you structure them?" Have participants take the post-its and cluster the department names together that could work as a team. Stand back and let them work through it. What you might find is the most common way that "non-ICS" teams are grouped:

- Facilities, Security, Safety
- IT
- Business Units
- Human Resources
- Finance Functions
- Communications
- Management

My, my, my. Doesn't that look a lot like ICS? (Just don't call it that.)

What do you look for in a leader?

In a crisis, strong leadership is a must. But what makes a good leader? If you're using the ICS structure, there must be an Incident Commander (IC). And each team needs a Team Leader as well.

Here are four essential requirements for leadership positions:

- Strong leadership skills
- Decisive, not afraid to make a decision
- Good overall understanding of the business
- Well respected by their peers and senior management

All of these are essential, especially the last one. If this person is unknown to senior management, or – worse yet – not respected, senior management may be inclined to step in and take over.

When looking at strong leadership skills, consider these top ten skills:[17]

1. **Communication** – able to clearly and succinctly explain to team members everything from organizational goals to specific tasks.

2. **Motivation** – is self-motivated and can motivate others.

3. **Delegation** – can identify the skills of employees and assign duties to each person based on his or her skill set.

4. **Positivity** – holds a positive attitude, which can go a long way in a crisis.

5. **Trustworthiness** – has integrity.

6. **Creativity** – is able to see things differently, can think "out of the box."

7 **Feedback** – can provide appropriate coaching and feedback to employees.

8. **Responsibility** – feels responsibility for both the successes and failures of his or her team and is willing to accept blame when something does not go correctly.

9. **Commitment** – follows through with what they agree to, stands by their words and decisions.

10. **Flexibility** – can accept whatever changes come their way.

Establish an executive briefing schedule

- Use the Incident Action Plan development timeframe as logical briefing times for Executive Management.

---

17   Doyle, Alison, "Top 10 Leadership Skills Leadership Skills Employers Look For", The Balance, June 8, 2017, https://www.thebalance.com/top-leadership-skills-2063782

66 *Hire people who are better than you are,*
then leave them to get on with it.
Look for people who will aim for the remarkable,
who will not settle for the routine. 99

— **David Ogilvy**
Founder Ogilvy & Mather

- Avoid holding briefings more often than every four hours. When meeting more often it can take too much of your precious time and it becomes difficult to determine status.
- A suggested schedule is after every Incident Action Plan meeting. If the operational periods are 12 hours, then a second briefing in the middle of the operational period is suggested.

For the other positions, those chosen should ideally have basic decision-making authority that is important for them to complete their role on the crisis team. They should also have a strong understanding of the business, the response and recovery plans, and, ideally, be well-trained and exercised.

Summary

Organizational structure provides clarity and process. Think of the crisis structure as the skeleton supporting the response efforts of the company. Each bone in the skeleton has a function, as does each team and role in the crisis process. Organizational structures help everyone know who does what. Creating a structure with clearly defined roles, functions, and scopes of authority and systems helps make sure your employees are working together to accomplish everything that must be done in the crisis. It is an important endeavor and worthy of your time and careful consideration.

CHAPTER 7

When to activate

Chapter topics

- *Activation criteria and severity level for incident assessment*
- *Incident Assessment Team process*
- *Executive briefing agenda and process*

66 *Teamwork is the ability to work together toward a common vision.*
The ability to direct individual accomplishments toward organizational objectives.
It is the fuel that allows common people to attain uncommon results. **99**

— Andrew Carnegie
19th century Industrialis

Introduction

Having a crisis management team is great, but how does the process actually unfold? When something happens in a department or a location, how does the event become known and evaluated? And once it's known, who evaluates the situation and what criteria do they use? If you have the answers to these questions, the processes will help you manage smaller things and prevent them from becoming a crisis. On the opposite end of the spectrum, these processes allow you to immediately jump on something that you know has the potential of seriously damaging your organization.

This part of the crisis management process is something that is missing in the vast majority of plans that we review or audit. The Bad Thing happens and then abracadabra! – like magic – the plan is activated! But wait a moment…how did that happen? Who made the decision to activate? What were the criteria? Was it codified or documented? The goal of this chapter is to explore a critical question: when do you activate?

When to activate

When an incident occurs, there are often a lot of assumptions about how and where information will be routed, who will be engaged, and how an activation will occur. When reviewing crisis plans, we have found the documentation is often completely silent on how to get from Point A (an incident occurs) to Point B (the plan is activated). It is critical to develop a clear incident assessment process for identifying who evaluates the situation and what criteria are used to activate (or not activate).

First, before we discuss the assessment process, there are three critical issues to review:

1. **Activation criteria:** These will guide the Incident Assessment Team in determining if plans should be activated.

2. **Incident levels:** This is a bit of shorthand to quickly describe an incident and its impact. Often shown as levels (1 through 3, or 1 through 5) or colors (red, yellow, green).

3. **Incident Assessment Team** (IAT): The team that will assess incidents and make the determination about what to do next.

Activation criteria

What's critical to your organization usually boils down to a few key things. In the beginning of our practice, activation checklists were fairly complex documents, full of many different things to consider and weigh. After years of practice, we have decided that simple is best. You don't need a lot of criteria to cover 99% of the issues you will face.

There are six issues the Incident Assessment Team should discuss to determine if an activation should occur:

1. Location of impact
2. Life Safety/People
3. Facilities
4. Information Technology/Information Security
5. Business/Time-sensitive activities at risk
6. Reputation/Brand

Location of impact

Looking quickly at the event's location determines the scope – whether it affects just your company or if others are also affected. For example, after an earthquake, responders will be slow to assist, employees will be slow (or unable) to respond, and critical infrastructure may not be available. Since we don't live in a bubble, however, even incidents that happen someplace else can still have a dramatic impact on the organization. For example, while there were only three locations in the United States where terrorist attacks occurred on 9/11, the entire country was deeply affected and essentially closed. An international event, like a bombing in another country, could impact you if you have locations nearby, or if your CEO is traveling there. To that end, you need to discuss four quick questions regarding the event's location:

- Is this a localized incident impacting your company only? (Example: fire in the building)
- Is this a regional incident? (Example: flooding, earthquake, massive windstorm, tsunami)
- Is this a national incident? (Example: terrorism, 9/11)
- Is this an international incident that spreads across countries or regions? (Example: tsunami, flooding, terrorism, earthquake, pandemic)

Life safety/ People

Once you understand the scope of the event based on its location, the next step should be to discuss people – your most critical asset.

- Is there a life safety issue?

- Is there an impact to your people? Are lives in danger or otherwise at risk? Have people been injured or killed?

Facilities

Next, find out what's happening with your facilities.

- Is one or more of your facilities at risk?
- Is there damage to any of your facilities?

Information technology/Information security

Next on the list to assess is technology:

- Is there a disruption of technology services (e.g., telecom, network, applications, data center)?
- Is there a potential Information Security issue? Intrusion? Breach?

Business/ time-sensitive activities at risk

Once you've determined the state of your technology, now it's time to move to the overall business:

- Does the situation have a significant (or potentially significant) impact to your time-sensitive business processes and/or operations? Which ones?
- Does the situation have a significant (or potentially significant) financial impact on your company?

Reputation / brand

And lastly, you must reflect on the more subjective but crucial, intangible part of the assessment: the impact or potential impact to your company's reputation or brand.

- Does the event risk harm to your organization's reputation or brand?

Qualitative approach

Some of our clients have wanted a more qualitative approach to this assessment and have developed a scale (i.e., 1 through 5) for each of the questions. They decide whether to activate or not based on the total score of the individual responses. If you choose to use this type of approach, you must decide the score that you feel would cause an activation, versus a score where you would only monitor the event. Personally, I think this tactic is fraught with peril, as a "5" score on reputation/brand or information technology could easily be serious enough to cause a crisis to the company even if the other scores are low. If your organization thinks along these lines, this might be appropriate. However, use this approach with caution and evaluate the total score carefully.

Using the five criteria areas below, rate each of the areas using a scale of 1 to 5 (least severe to most severe).

Example

In the example below, the company total for this event is 20. In the company's activation guidelines, it would have defined what "20" meant, either "activate" or "monitor.."

INCIDENT ASSESSMENT

Location	Life Safety/ People	Facilities	Information Technology / Information Security	Business/ Time-sensitive Activities at Risk	Reputation/ Brand	Total
Localized incident						
Regional incident						
National incident						
International incident						

Ratings: "**1**" would equal "minor impact.
"**2**" would equal "**minimal impact.**
"**3**" would equal "moderate impact

"**4**" would equal "serious impact.
"**5**" would equal "catastrophic impact.

Incident Levels

You may already use incident levels as a means of shorthand to describe the impact of an incident. Technology teams have been using incident levels for many years. For example, if

INCIDENT ASSESSMENT

Location	Life Safety/ People	Facilities	Information Technology / Information Security	Business/ Time-sensitive Activities at Risk	Reputation/ Brand	Total
Localized incident	3	5	5	4	3	20

Ratings: "**1**" would equal "minor impact.
"**2**" would equal "minimal impact.
"**3**" would equal "moderate impact

"**4**" would equal "serious impact.
"**5**" would equal "catastrophic impact.

you speak of an incident as a "Level 1" to someone familiar with the incident level nomenclature, they immediately have an understanding of the impact. It is a helpful, quick tool to get everybody on board with the problem.

Before you develop or revise your incident levels, however, be sure to check with your technology department. I advocate that your levels should be the "same direction" as theirs. In other words, if "Severity Level 1" in your Technology department is the most severe, make your "Level 1" be the most severe level as well. This just makes it easier for everyone to know that a "Level 1" incident means that the situation is "really bad."

The following sample matrix not only reviews the Incident Level but also notes who is responsible and defines the basic communications and notifications.

Incident Assessment Team

I'll first talk about the Incident Assessment Team (IAT) at the corporate offices. We always start with the "mothership" (i.e., corporate) and then expand out from there.

Members of the corporate
Incident Assessment Team (IAT)

An IAT is often comprised of key individuals in departments where most of the incidents likely occur. This includes facilities, security, and technology. The Incident Commander is most commonly included in the assessment team, and perhaps representatives of key lines of Business, Communications, or Human Re-

Level	Impact	Example	Responsibility	Communications / Notifications
SEVERITY LEVEL 1 (S1) **Catastrophic**	Catastrophic	• Major earthquake, explosion, fire or other event that seriously damages your company buildings and/or killing people. • Data Center down – catastrophic failure of a DC, unable to process out of that site. • Technology/cyber, inability to function.	• Incident Assessment Team notified. • Crisis Management Team activated. • Emergency Operations Center activated. • Executive Management activated.	• Incident Assessment Team activates Crisis Management Team. • Communication issued to all employees, key stakeholders depending on the impact. • External stakeholders. • Executive Management. • Board.

Level	Impact	Example	Responsibility	Communications / Notifications
SEVERITY LEVEL 2 (S2) **Immediate response**	Moderate to severe	• Sustained impact to your company facility affecting one or more buildings due to fire, flood, earthquake, protracted unexpected power disruption, etc. • Release of hazardous chemicals on nearby freeway, with an impact to your company. • Workplace violence. • Terrorism affecting region. • Technology/cyber incident making it difficult to perform critical functions.	• Incident Assessment Team notified. • Crisis Management Team activated. • Emergency Operations Center activated. • Executive Management notified.	• Incident Assessment Team activates Crisis Management Team. • Communication issued to all employees, key suppliers, and contractors. • External stakeholders as necessary. • Executive Management.

Level	Impact	Example	Responsibility	Communications / Notifications
SEVERITY LEVEL 3 (S3) **Incident Limited in scope**	Limited in scope	• Small fire with limited damage. • Unexpected short-term power outage. • Short term technology outage.	• Managed as business as usual by affected departments.	• Notification through usual means, handled by affected department. • Incident Assessment Team may be notified by department managing the incident as an FYI.
SEVERITY LEVEL 4 (S4) **Minor incident departments**	Minor, no disruption	• Medical emergency. • Minor security incident. • Minor technology issues w/acceptable workarounds available • Minor weather event, no damage.	• Managed as business as usual.	• Notification as necessary through usual means, handled by affected department.

sources. It really depends on your previous history, company specifics, culture, and experience.

- Mandatory members:
  - Facilities
  - Security
  - Technology
  - Incident Commander
- Optional members (these people can always be called in if the situation warrants it):
  - Key lines of business
  - Communications
  - Human Resources

The IAT is a temporary team. If the IAT makes the decision to activate the Corporate Crisis Management Team (CCMT) and plan, then they "fold into" the CCMT and no longer exist as a separate team. The IAT is only in the business of assessment and activation decisions. Once that is done, they return to their usual CCMT role.

Incident Assessment Team at other locations

All locations need an Incident Assessment Team regardless of size. There needs to be a group of individuals at every location organization-wide with the responsibility for conducting an assessment and then doing the appropriate notifications.

For example, in a small facility, members of the Crisis Management Team and the Incident Assessment Team are likely the same people. The key thing to remember is that there should be a group of people who are pre-identified and who understand their role. In the event of an emergency, they know to assemble, make an assessment, and then notify the appropriate individuals to whom they report.

Business Unit/Department Incident Assessment Teams

There are likely "assessment-style" teams in a variety of business units and departments, such as Technology. When an IT outage occurs, they would activate their Incident Management process. If there is a major business impact, they need to notify the Corporate IAT for further company-wide assessment. Another example is an insurance company with Catastrophic Response Teams. In a major incident (such as during hurricanes Harvey or Irma), the activation of those teams will have major business impacts across the company. The activation of those teams should automatically trigger a notification to the Corporate IAT. Business units and departments with those types of assessment teams and processes need to include in their documentation the notification of the Corporate IAT for Severity Level 1 and 2 incidents.

Availability

IAT members must be "always" on call, as an incident could happen at any time. They need to be able to jump on a call, obtain situational awareness about the incident, discuss it with their colleagues, and then make a decision to activate the plan or monitor the situation. These IAT members should have a company-issued mobile device as well as provide their home phone number for ac-

*66 Individual commitment to a group effort –
that is what makes a team work,
a company work, a society work. 99*

— **Vince Lombardi**
Legendary football coach

cess any time of day or night.

IAT Notification

The goal is simplicity: Make it easy for issues to get reported so the IAT can be brought in to conduct an assessment. Hopefully your company has an Emergency Notification System (ENS)[18]. Having an ENS allows you to set up an IAT group, as well as groups for all the crisis management teams, key departments, specialized groups, and all employees.

If you have a 24-hour Security Operations Center (SOC), you can use its phone number as the primary number for employees to call and report incidents. Any of your organization's assessment teams would then be trained to call it when an incident occurs. The SOC would then notify the Corporate IAT of the incident (presumably using the ENS), instructing IAT members to join a phone bridge for a briefing regarding an incident.

---

18   Among other things, an emergency notification system (ENS) is a method of facilitating the one-way dissemination or broadcast of messages to one or many groups of people, alerting them to a pending or existing emergency.

Incident assessment process

At this point you should have the following three things determined:

1. Activation criteria
2. Incident levels
3. Incident Assessment Team membership

Now we can talk about the assessment process. A simple flow from incident awareness to plan activation usually includes six steps:

1. **Awareness.** An individual Incident Assessment Team member becomes aware of an incident through a variety of means. If it could disrupt a time-sensitive business processes and/or is a life safety issue, the team member then goes immediately to step 2.

2. **Assembly.** In the event that the Incident Assessment Team member feels the incident may be significant, s/he will activate the full Incident Assessment Team, which then performs a formal assessment using the activation criteria and the severity levels matrix.

3. **Decision.** The Incident Assessment Team decides if the plan will be activated by asking the question out loud, "Should we activate?"

4. **Activate.** The organization's Crisis Management Plan is activated. Notify Executives of the plan activation and that a formal briefing will occur after the IAP meeting.

5. **Plan.** The team develops an Incident Action Plan.
6. **Brief.** Executives are briefed on the incident.

The following section is what you would expect to see in your Crisis Management plan, walking through the six steps with some detail and clear action steps.

Awareness

The first Incident Assessment Team member who becomes aware of an incident will assess the situation and, if appropriate, notify the team. Most incidents are likely to come from one of these departments: Facilities, Security, Information Technology, or Information Security. Any incident will follow the normal chain-of-command until it reaches an Incident Assessment Team member.

Key aspects of the process include:

- Incidents will be reported through the usual reporting structure.
- Events that are likely to cause an activation of the Crisis Management Plan will be made known to the Incident Assessment Team (or their designee), which will initiate the assessment process via the Emergency Notification System.
- Any member of the Incident Assessment Team has the authority and responsibility to activate the Emergency Notification System to gather the rest of the Incident Assessment Team.

The Incident Assessment Team member's responsibilities include notifying the Incident Assessment Team:

- Any member of the company's Incident Assessment Team who becomes aware of an incident that may materially interfere with the company's operations (level S1 or S2) should immediately notify the other Incident Assessment Team members by using the Emergency Notification System, group text, or telephone tree.
- Smaller events (level S3 or less) will be handled by the departments assigned to them. These events will likely not rise up to the level of the Incident Assessment Team, *however*, if in any doubt, the discovering IAT member should notify the Incident Assessment Team and assess the situation.

Assembly

The full IAT meets (either face-to-face or by conference call) to assess the incident and assign an incident level and make an activation decision. Here is what you need to detail in your plan:

Virtual meeting information

Spell out very clearly how the virtual meeting will work:

- Describe your mechanism of getting the IAT on a phone bridge. Be specific about whether you will use an emergency notification system (ENS), group text, or make individual phone calls.

- Document your phone bridge number and host and participant codes.

Physical meeting locations

List these in order of preference:

- Primary/Internal: <<note meeting location>>
- Secondary (if the office is not physically accessible): <<note meeting location>>
- Tertiary (used only if the primary and secondary locations are not accessible): <<note meeting location>>

Incident Assessment Team meeting agenda

- Take roll. Determine who is in charge of the call and who is taking notes.
- Share information. The person with the situational awareness of the incident shares the incident with the team.
  - Decide if you need to bring any other subject matter experts into the discussion.
  - Determine if you have all the information or sources that you need.
- Review the Incident Assessment Activation Criteria to assess the incident.
- Assign an incident level.

Make the decision

At last, it's the moment of truth. This is referred to as "calling the question." Ask the question out loud, "Do we activate the Crisis Management Plan and the team?" If the answer is yes, go to the next step, activation. If the answer is no, assign an IAT member to monitor the situation and keep the team informed until the issue is resolved.

Activate

The IAT uses the Activation Process Checklist to activate the plan and the team.

- Note: At the point of activation, the IAT becomes part of the full crisis team
- Notify the Executives that a plan activation has occurred, and they will receive a full briefing following the IAP meeting

Activation checklist

This quick reference checklist lists all critical actions that should be completed immediately once the Crisis Management Plan is activated. This is accomplished in three simple steps.

Activation step #1: Determine the Emergency Operations Center (EOC) location.

Determine which EOC location will be activated (listed in order of preference and availability):

- Primary/Internal: <<note meeting location>>
- Secondary (if the office is not physically accessible): <<note meeting location>>
- Tertiary (used only if the primary and secondary locations are not accessible): <<note meeting location>>

Activation Step #2: Activate the team members; make immediate notifications.

- Activate the Crisis Management Team
- Initiate call tree/Emergency Notification System with situation status/details, as appropriate
- Update Employee Hotline <<note number here>>
- Notify Executive Management and provide them with a brief situation summary (a detailed briefing will happen after the first Incident Action Planning session is held)

Activation Step #3: Get organized; review Crisis Management Team checklists.

- Go to the Crisis Management Plan and review the checklists for the teams being activated
- Define initial staffing requirements
- Determine team logistics (food, equipment, and any urgent support)

Plan

An Incident Action Planning (IAP) meeting is held as soon as the Incident Management Plan is activated and the team convenes.

- A briefing is held, objectives are developed, and the operational period (time to the next meeting) is determined
- Begin the IAP meeting with an update on the situation status
- Hold further IAP meetings at the end of each operational period

Essential elements in any IAP include:

- **Strategic objectives.** Answer the question, "What are we expected to achieve?" Think of this as a to-do list. Objectives should be high-level, prioritized, and consistent with company policy

- **Assignments to accomplish the objectives.** Answer the question, "*Who* will do *what, when,* and *where*?" Assignments include employee assignments necessary to perform the required functions to meet the objectives

- **Operational period (OP).** Determine the operational period (when the next meeting will occur). If the situation is quite intense, the first OP may be short – one-to-two hours. Objectives are written for this time frame, and there's a briefing at the conclusion of the OP.

The process of developing an IAP will be covered in detail in chapter 12.

Brief

The sixth and final step of assessment and plan activation is to brief Executive Management. A detailed briefing can occur after the first Incident Action Plan has been developed. Be sure to bring any critical subject matter experts required for complete information. The following briefing agenda can be used for the initial and on-going briefings.

EXECUTIVE BRIEFING AGENDA

High level overview of the incident. Focus briefing on impacts to:

- People
- Company facilities and technology
- Time-sensitive business processes
- Reputation and brand

Key actions underway to manage the crisis.

Communications

(this can be simply a report out or a discussion on strategy):

- Employees
- Key stakeholders (list all here)
- Traditional media
- Social media

What we need from you.

- List all actions the crisis management team needs from Executive Management. Focus on their specific roles:
  - Decisions: making policies or strategic decisions
  - Funding: approving funding for recovery issues
  - Acting as senior relationship manager: Reaching out to any organizations or individuals deemed critical such as large customers, Board members, regulators, government officials
  - Acting as media spokesperson: only if requested by Communications

Next meeting date/time/location or update.

Establish an executive briefing schedule

- Use the Incident Action Plan development timeframe as logical briefing times for Executive Management.
- Avoid holding briefings more often than every four hours. When meeting more often it can take too much of your precious time and it becomes difficult to determine status.
- A suggested schedule is after every Incident Action Plan meeting. If the operational periods are 12 hours, then a second briefing in the middle of the operational period is suggested.

Summary

Incident assessment is one of the most important, yet overlooked, aspects of crisis management. Working through this process will do more to improve your organization's ability to manage an incident in the initial stages than anything else. Commit to working through this material to dramatically improve your resiliency.

CHAPTER 8

Where do you convene?

Chapter topics

- *Virtual Emergency Operations Centers offer flexibility and require special planning and preparation*
- *Physical Emergency Operations Centers are essential in incidents where power and internet connectivity are impacted*
- *All companies need to have the ability to operate in both the physical and virtual realm*

❝ *The time to repair the roof is when the sun is shining.* **❞**

— **John F Kennedy**
35th President of the United States
State of the Union address,
January 11, 1962

Introduction

To paraphrase Shakespeare, "To meet physically or not to meet physically, that is the question…" Historically, Emergency Operations Centers (EOC) were always at a specific location with everyone physically together. In the last few years, the growth of collaboration and project management tools (software and applications) has really expanded virtual EOC possibilities. Of course, both a physical EOC and a virtual one require power and internet connectivity.

All organizations must be very familiar with their risk assessment profile in order to make a wise choice regarding the type of command center it selects. The company needs to know what challenges it is most likely to face to make that decision. In areas where regional disasters are in the mix – like earthquakes or hurricanes – a company needs to have solid plans for both options. This chapter looks at both virtual and physical command centers and how to make either of them successful.

Where to meet

I'm sure most of us have been on a crisis conference call. What do you think of them? I often find them frustrating. People drop on and off, or they come in late and need to be brought up to speed. Participants are distracted by other things on their communication devices or at their desks and don't pay attention. Still others are multitasking, and their focus is elsewhere. Worse, decisions are often made with incomplete information. Unless the person who is driving the meeting has a virtual whip, the results tend to be less desirable than at a face-to-face meeting.

If holding a normal conference call were the only way you could run a virtual command center, I would say, "Fuhged-daboudit!" It's not an effective way to run a crisis. However, things are changing, and there are now many formal virtual EOC software options available. I encourage you to approach having a physical or virtual EOC with an open mind.

Virtual EOC

As collaboration and project management software and applications continue to be developed and become more robust, having a virtual EOC is becoming more and more of a viable option. Of course, you still must have power and internet connectivity to make them work.

If you opt to go the virtual route, here are some of the virtues

1. Virtual works for many incidents. Many incidents can be handled virtually or physically. Smaller incidents (i.e., a limited IT outage or a snow day) give you an opportunity to try out a virtual set-up.

2. Everybody has the same information. There is far less of a chance of people not knowing what is going on. Incident Action Plans can be placed on the platform everyone is working on. Likewise, images or video of the incident can be displayed to all. Break-out chat rooms can be formed for instant collaboration.

3. Virtual EOCs eliminate the need for staffing a large physical space. For small companies/departments and geo-

graphically-dispersed workforces, this can be a real plus.

4. No one has to travel to participate – a big plus in many situations.

5. Information sharing is easier. You can get people to the table faster. Everyone can hear and see the same thing. It also allows for easier tracking and resolution of issues.

6. Minimal training required for participants.

7. Easy to set up and maintain.

What to look for in a Virtual Emergency Operations Center

Here's a short list of what you should look for when researching collaboration and project management software and applications:

- Collaborative workspaces
- Status boards
- Message feeds
- Task and time tracking
- Board views (boards to visualize the flow of tasks and activities)
- Repository for plans, documents, image.

The good news about these types of software and applications is that there are many possible uses for them in your organization, not just as a virtual EOC. They are relatively easy to learn, are hosted in the cloud so they will not be affected by a data center outage, and most of them are cost-effective. This is much better than the old days of clunky and cumbersome Emergency Operations Center software. The best way to understand these new tools is to try them out. Many of the main providers offer free 60-day trials and online training.

Here are some of the most popular to date:

- Asana https://asana.com/
- Basecamp https://basecamp.com/
- Liquid Planner https://www.liquidplanner.com/
- Mavenlink https://start.mavenlink.com
- Podio https://podio.com/site
- Teamwork https://www.teamwork.com/project-management-software
- Wrike https://try.wrike.com

Physical EOC

When setting up a physical Emergency Operations Center, whether primary, secondary, or tertiary (if applicable), you need to first look at your risk profile and identify your likely risks.

Many of the comments and information in this section can also be applied to setting up a virtual EOC, such as establishing status boards, staffing, scheduling, and organization.

Where to meet

First, identify where to locate your physical command center. At a minimum, you need two locations, identified in advance:

- Primary: In your building, as long as there is sufficient space to accommodate your full team. Training rooms are often the best options.

- Secondary: Outside of your building, in case it is damaged, as long as you can get to it within a reasonable amount of travel time, based on your risk profile. This could be a hotel meeting room.

Reviewing your risk profile will help you decide how far away your secondary EOC needs to be from your primary site, and whether you need to select a tertiary site as well. For example, if you have earthquakes defined as a risk, your secondary site needs to take into account the likely forecasted damage to critical infrastructure (such as transportation and utilities), as well as where the majority of your employees live. As another example, if you are located within 50 miles of a nuclear power plant or are in an area which has a threat from nuclear or chemical weapons (such as Washington, D.C.), then you need a tertiary site that takes into account distance and "prevailing winds."

Process and staffing

One thing that most companies don't think about is how to organize the team and command center. Addressing this in advance is critical to ensure that the team can hit the ground running and not get bogged down in "who does what and when?"

Start with the basics - how the physical room will be organized and set up. Is there one large table or multiple smaller tables? One large table is not recommended. By the very nature of group dynamics, having everyone sit around one large table means the team is acting as a single unit. This inhibits smaller teams (also sitting at the big table) from working together effectively, which is an essential component to managing a crisis. That's why several smaller tables - three or four – are more productive

Once you've addressed the physical set-up of the room, the next issue to address is how you will display information. In a crisis situation, information can come from many sources. In many fast-moving emergencies, people have described the amount of information coming at them as "like drinking out of a fire hose." You need to think about how you display information, so it can be seen and digested by everyone who needs to see it. This can be accomplished with something as simple as a flip chart, or go high-tech and have display screens available.

Next, think about your staffing plans. You will need people to do all kinds of things – make phone calls or copies, run errands, write on status boards, take notes, track down people or things, and more. Identify in advance what administrative support is available and determine ways they can be helpful.

Information display

In a physical EOC, having a place to display information – whether it's electronic (screen) or a flipchart on an easel or a whiteboard – is essential to track status. This includes the "static facts" of the incident (facts that don't change), as well as team activities or specifics such as an IT "dashboard" (describing the status of specific services, applications, networks, etc.)

Each Emergency Operations Center team should maintain its own status board for information that is pertinent to their activities and concerns. The Incident Commander should be able to glance up at the boards and get a complete picture of the event. The following posting suggestions can be used as a guide.

Information should be color-coded as a quick visual aid. For example, put action items in **RED** and informational items in **BLACK.** Include the date and time of all notations. If multiple people are allowed to update the board, also include the initials of the person who entered the information.

For continuity, assign one or two persons to maintain the status board.

If also using a virtual tool, set it up to do these tasks.

General Status Board (static information)

The general status board has the more static information about the event, noting things such as overall impact and local infrastructure outages. This board should include event data such as date and time of incident, high-level overview of incident, global statistics, and basic core facts.

Regional Status Board

In regional events, regional status boards should be established to track damage to infrastructure such as transportation lifelines (highways, bridges, freeways, airports, public transportation), utilities (electric, gas, water, sewer), as well as government responses.

Operations Status Board

Due to the nature of Operations, this group's board reflects the basic status of the event and the tactical response to it:

- Current status and response to the incident
- Technology: Platforms, network, telecom, data, servers
  - If possible, display this information in a dashboard format using colors for fast recognition. Consider using green to mean "operational," yellow to mean "there are issues," and red to mean "down."

Communications Status Board

Communications' board will reflect the status of:
- Approved talking points
- Media briefing schedules
- Traditional media: Statements and press releases, clippings or links to stories
- Social media: Statements and press releases, samples of postings (good and bad)

Human Resources Status Board

Since Human Resources' focus is on the general welfare of people, both at the affected site and at the EOC, their board should contain the following information:
- People, injuries, fatalities (Keep names confidential by assigning numbers to casualties)
- Human Resources issues, needs and requests, and responses

Finance Status Board

Finance will focus on financial and insurance-related issues. Their board should reflect the following:

- Payroll status
- Procurement needs/orders
- Disaster account information
- Insurance status and issues

Planning Status Board

Planning status boards should note recovery issues and concerns about the status of the recovery.

Sample Emergency Operations Center set-up checklist

Upon instruction from the Incident Commander or their designee, the Business Continuity Department or their designee will set up the Emergency Operations Center. Use the following checklist during the setup process:

- Obtain office and other supplies and bring to designated command center
- Distribute supplies at each table
- If necessary, connect telephones (unless using mobiles)
- Test all telephones
- Place a set of "white-board friendly" markers at each white board
- Update two clocks on the wall:
  - Clock 1: Local time
  - Clock 2: Elapsed time since the start of the emergency
- Display map of emergency area and blueprints of emergency site (if available)
- Arrange for and install any needed equipment, such as

photocopiers or printers

- Have an LCD projector available for briefings as necessary
- Have extra surge protectors and tape to secure cords in the room
- Document time and number of persons involved in set-up
- Organize an EOC break and rest area
- Set up an EOC catering area. Place sign above table reading, "No eating in the Emergency Operations Center"
- Place at least one large trashcan by catering table
- Provide bottled water 24 hours a day

Sample Emergency Operations Center shut-down checklist

Once the Emergency Operations Center has been deactivated, a careful shutdown process is essential to prevent loss of valuable information and equipment. Use the following checklist during the shutdown process:

- Store EOC documentation per the company's document retention policy
- Return borrowed equipment
- Carefully fold and re-package re-usable items, such as maps and charts
- Box all directories, plans, books, forms, and other resources
- Perform inventory of supplies:
  - Attach a list of missing EOC supplies

- ○ Attach a list of needed additional EOC supplies
- ○ Provide the EOC Manager with list of additional and replacement Emergency Operations Center supplies
- Make sure that the workspace is left reasonably clean and in good order
- Wipe down all white boards
- Collect all logs, reports, message forms, and other significant documentation related to the incident (Check with your Legal team or department to determine which materials to save and how long they should be kept)
- Scan documents as necessary for electronic storage
- Break room or rest area:
  - ○ Clean break area and have food services remove items such as coffee pots, as necessary
  - ○ Arrange with Facilities to have trashcans emptied throughout the Emergency Operations Center
  - ○ Re-supply cases of bottled water used during the Emergency Operations Center activation.

❝ *Great things in business are never done by one person; they're done by a team of people.* **❞**

— **Steve Jobs**
Apple co-founder

SUGGESTED ITEMS FOR THE EOC FACILITY

Item/ Feature	Number	Location	Comments
Directional signs for each function in and out baskets			
Supply box for each team table including basic office supplies, forms, plans and any equipment specifically requested by the team			
Wall clocks			
Area maps for each strategic location			
Floor plans of each facility impacted			
Telephones for each function			
Pads of lined paper			
Highlighters			
Post-it notes			
Printer			
Copier (or note location of closest)			
Television/cable or internet connection			
Conference telephone			
AM/FM radio			
Cell phones, chargers, extra batteries			
Business unit continuity plans			

SUGGESTED ITEMS FOR THE EOC FACILITY

Item/ Feature	Number	Location	Comments
Crisis management plan			
Telephone books			
Two long tables for catering			
Large trash cans for catering table			
Small trash cans for each table			
First aid kit			

PERSONAL SUPPLIES FOR THE EOC TEAM MEMBERS

Item / Feature	Number	Location	Comments
Pre-made personal hygiene packages for EOC staff (shampoo, toothbrush, toothpaste, soap)			
Chlorine bleach (1 gallon)			
Trash bags			
Blankets/pillows (for rest area)			
Hand sanitizer wipes or gel (60% alcohol)			
Bottled water			

Summary

It is critical to figure out in advance how you will operate your command center. Many organizations never consider this before an activation and then stumble for the first few hours, or even days, after an incident. Explore your options. The wave of the future is a virtual Emergency Operations Center. At the same time, don't completely abandon a physical EOC. There are many types of crises where you will need one to succeed.

CHAPTER 9

Why an effective crisis management program is important

Chapter topics

- *Ways to advance your crisis program by talking about value*
- *Eight ways to explore value in your crisis management program*
- *Marketing crisis management in your organization*

66 *In preparing for battle I have always found that plans are useless, but planning is indispensable.* 99

— **Dwight D. Eisenhower**
36th President of the
United States of America

Introduction

To paraphrase the English poet Elizabeth Barrett Browning, "Why is an effective crisis management program important? Let me count the ways." I believe most people intuitively understand and know why crisis management preparation is important. Yet, for many companies, the risk appetite for such planning and readiness has decreased, even in the face of significant threats and risks.

If/when you talk about the potential loss of revenue or the impact to the brand and reputation of the organization, the chances are you are often met with, "Yes, but when did that last happen to us and how did we do?" If you are like most organizations, disasters and crises don't happen very often (thankfully), so you may not have much of a comeback. That kind of vague response doesn't motivate executives to spend the money or the time to build a good program. Robust crisis management is about investing and protecting your future – think of it as insurance. This chapter provides some verbal ammunition for you to use.

Why is an effective crisis management program important?

A crisis is any event that threatens your company. Crisis management protects the organization's core mission and business and can help to protect its reputation and brand. Unfortunately, sometimes that's a hard sell. One of the biggest challenges someone charged with overseeing a crisis management program has to overcome is to prove that the program is worth its investment to the company. If you don't have a lot of crises to point to, however, how can you convince others that an effective program is a strategic imperative to protect your company's assets, its brand and its people?

The "dreaded question" of return-on-investment (ROI)

"What is your program's ROI?" is what I call the "dreaded question." So, here's how the questions are often framed:

- "What's the return on investment (ROI) of your crisis planning efforts?"
- "How much money will you save the company?"
- "How much money will you make for the company?"
- "What does this do to the company's bottom line?"

Answering these questions can get really tricky. There are several ways to address the ROI question...but first, start with some soul-searching on your part.

1. First of all, ask yourself: Do you have a compelling crisis management program – one that defines and addresses the top risks and essential strategies to thwart or mitigate them? Can you frame the risks in a manner to make ignoring them unthinkable? Can you summarize them in less than a minute to a C-suite executive who happens to be in the elevator with you and asks you whether crisis management is really a strategic imperative?

2. Once you have honed those answers, try them out on your boss. Indeed, work with her/him in fine-tuning those talking points. Ask for suggestions. Reach accord on the best

way to tell your story. This does two things: (1) it helps you sharpen your pitch while (2) implicitly preparing your boss to support you and your program when he is challenged in some executive meeting.

3.   Manage up your chain-of-command. Work with your boss to make sure your management is wholly on-board with your goals, strategies and recommendations. Brief her/him carefully so s/he really understands and supports your mission and your strategies. Be sure that s/he has the ammunition they need to discuss the program and its merits at a moment's notice.

Answering the ROI question

One way to answer is to point to other companies that have done poorly when faced with a significant crisis and attempt to extrapolate the situation to your organization. That may sound good, but you are likely to get a second question, "What is the likelihood of that happening to us?" That's tough to answer when you lack a crystal ball.

"ROI" stands for "return on investment." That means that you need to prove that the organization received the same amount of money back – or more – as it invested in your program. You can point to your Business Impact Analysis (BIA), point to your planning efforts, correlate the two – and pray for the best. If a serious outage occurred, it's a pretty easy argument because you can show how the company is better off for having a crisis program. However, if you're like many crisis professionals, you likely have had no disasters or plan activations, or – even more problematical – the situations you faced were easy.

You will likely lose with that kind of response.

What if you changed the entire conversation? In other words, what if you started to talk about something more meaningful, like **value?** The questions I'd like to pose here are:

- What is the value-add of crisis management?
- Is that value-add only good in a disaster?
- *Is there a way to show value to the organization on a daily basis?*

Another approach: Value on investment (VOI)

Is it possible to tie dollars invested to desired – and realistic – company outcomes such as:

- Increased resiliency?
- Competitive advantage?
- Effective employee training?
- More thoughtful business processes?

Overwhelmingly, the answer is 'yes,' and to do that, we now need to discuss value and Value on Investment (VOI).

Value on investment was first defined by the Gartner Group[19], which described it as the *intangible assets that contribute heavily to an organization's performance.* The keyword there is *intangible.* These intangible assets include knowledge, processes, organizational structure, and ability to collaborate – which is what crisis

---

19   Roberts, John, "The Elusive Business Value of IT," Gartner, August 2002, https://www.gartner.com/doc/365685/elusive-business-value-it

management is all about! So VOI is the measure of the intangible benefits of a project or an activity. And just by the very nature of things, VOI will include some aspects of ROI – but that's not where you want to end up. You will want to talk about *value.*

Shifting to a VOI approach instead of an ROI approach provides the necessary forward-thinking framework for scoping, prioritizing, and initiating crisis projects. For example, in response to the executive's question, what if you said this instead: *"We use the concept of VOI because we are working to measure the idea of creating company resilience, of tying planning outcomes to increased response skills, and of creating value through collaborative planning and learning at every level of the organization."* Wow, that sounds great!

VOI helps measure the total value of "soft," or intangible, benefits derived from crisis initiatives, in addition to those "hard" benefits measured by ROI. VOI is, of course, subjective and would be difficult to measure with the same precision as ROI. Yet a VOI approach is critical to gaining funding for crisis planning efforts that provide the competitive difference necessary for the success of the efforts.

And, by the way, crisis professionals aren't the only ones who struggle with this. When you research this topic (VOI versus ROI), you will find many groups working through the same questions, including organizations and programs such as higher education, not-for-profits, professional associations, think tanks, and technology initiatives. You are not alone!

The first step begins with changing the conversation, moving it away from ROI to VOI. There are many ways to do that; one of my favorite ways is to spend some deep and quality time discussing three basic questions:

- "What is the company crisis management program doing now that provides value to the company?"
- "What should the crisis management program begin doing that would provide additional value to the company?"
- "What [am I/are we] doing to provide value to the company?"

One way to start getting your arms around the answers to these questions is to have what we call a *"whiteboard activity."* The whole purpose is to expand and deepen your thinking about what the program is doing now and/or could do and identify what everyone is doing to contribute to the success of the program's mission.

Here are some ways to set up a great brainstorming environment to capture ideas. These will help make that whiteboard activity really pop:

1. Establish goals for the session.
2. Set a timeline for the session.
3. Give everyone on your team a homework assignment: Bring to the session at least ten ways that the program provides value. They can be silly ones, great ones, boring ones – bring any and all of them!
4. Create an environment for success. Be prepared at the start of the meeting with sketchpads, sticky notes, colored

markers and a large amount of whiteboard space for everyone involved.

5. Write down and/or sketch out every idea. *Every* idea, good or bad, should be presented.
6. Don't judge. Embrace the ridiculous or crazy ideas. At the end of the day, it might be the best idea in the room.
7. Start with general topics and then move toward the specific.
8. Look for synergy among the ideas. There is often potential for creating synergy among originally separate suggestions.
9. Don't fall in love with your ideas. Shop them around and see how they hold up.

Viola! You are making progress.

Eight Ideas on VOI

To jump-start your thinking, here are eight different ways that your program might provide VOI. (Don't pull these out until your team has finished doing their own brainstorming first!)

1. Regulatory or contractual compliance
2. Competitive advantage
3. Brand and reputation protection
4. Risk identification
5. Risk awareness and assessment
6. Knowledge capture
7. Increased robustness
8. Deeper knowledge

Idea #1: Regulatory or contractual compliance

An obvious value-add is one that is required by your profession, such as the Federal Financial Institutions Examination Council (FFIEC) guidelines for the banking industry. The FFIEC Business Continuity Planning Booklet is very specific.

> "Business continuity planning should include the development of a crisis management team and crisis management process. The key to a good crisis management team is in the planning. Individuals should be able to make instantaneous decisions, possibly based on limited information, often without the support of others. Each recovery scenario requires a specific media plan and notification plan as well. The BCP allows the institution to recover critical business operations, and the crisis management team deals with the crisis at hand. A crisis management test can be used to validate the overall process, including disaster declaration and escalation procedures."[20]

However, you may not be in an industry or profession that is subject to requirements from external regulators. If that's the case, you might think to yourself that this idea doesn't apply. Hold on, though – let's think about this more deeply. Regulatory compli-

---

20   "Business Continuity Planning Booklet, Crisis Management", FFIEC, https://
     ithandbook.ffiec.gov/it-booklets/business-continuity-planning/other-policies,-
     standards-and-processes/crisis-management.aspx

ance might not be a requirement for your company, but it could be a requirement for one of your big customers. For example, take the FFIEC Appendix J requirement, "Strengthening the Resilience of Outsourced Technology Services." This requires that third-party vendors meet certain requirements for planning and testing. Are you one of those third-party vendors who need to meet certain requirements? Or maybe there is a contractual requirement from a customer in order for them to do business with your company. Your excellent program meets their requirements, and therefore your company can do business with them.

Or you could look at it this way – you are trying to set yourself apart from your competitors and you want to highlight your resilience, continuity planning, and crisis management as a selling point, which – conveniently – leads us to idea #2.

Idea #2: Competitive Advantage

Most organizations and companies prefer to do business with businesses that have a well-known reputation for delivering products and services on time. But delivering products and services on time also includes doing that when a disaster has happened at your facility. Your customers may be empathetic, but they still want their widget and/or service on time.

In addition, having a comprehensive and tested business continuity and crisis management program assures customers of your ability to deliver on the mutually-agreed-upon SLAs and thereby demonstrates value to them.

And lastly, your competitors may not even have a program, or one not as robust as yours, and you can highlight that in sales presentations.

Idea #3: Brand and Reputation Protection

Every organization needs to be prepared for what to do when something goes very wrong. In today's world, with the continuous news cycle and when anyone can become a reporter and post to social media, you cannot be caught flat-footed in your response. Your organization's inability to respond in a timely manner demonstrating your competence can result in lost customers, loss of market share, loss of investor confidence, suppliers distancing themselves from you, and the emergence of investor activists on your Board.

Think about it: having a comprehensive crisis management program helps protect your organization from the negative publicity that could result from a disruption to your operations. It's a great thing for your business to be known for reliability and integrity in spite of a serious outage.

You can't prevent every crisis or disaster from occurring, but you can mitigate the negative impact by having in place a plan, team, and process to handle them. And if – or more likely, when – the "Bad Thing" happens, your crisis management team will have a great story of resilience to tell, instead of an "Oops!" story.

Idea #4: Risk identification

Crisis management works hand-in-hand with Enterprise Risk Management. When you perform hazard risk and business impact

66 *Your brand isn't what you say it is,*
it's what Google says it is. **99**

— Chris Anderson
British-American author
and entrepreneur

analyses across all physical locations and within each process or function, and with your customers, threats and vulnerabilities will always be discovered. This critical risk identification, then, allows the organization to mitigate the risk where possible and prepare for the risk by developing plans and conducting exercises and training to improve response performance.

Every time you discover a risk, you have the opportunity to make operational changes or physical enhancements that will reduce or eliminate the possibility of some or most of the organizational risks. This saves money at the time of a disaster but may also contribute to insurance savings on an annual basis.

Despite a solid risk management process, there will still be problems that occur because it is impossible to predict all crisis events and protect against them. Your crisis management program will help prepare you to deal with the crisis and take action immediately – identifying and assessing issues and options and developing the appropriate response. Having the right risk management processes in place will give you a leg up in managing through any crisis.

Idea #5: Risk awareness and assessment

When you develop crisis plans, you may discover that the greatest value of a comprehensive crisis management program and process is *awareness*. This is awareness that is gained from examining potential risks, exploring what could happen, deciding who needs to assess and manage the situation, examining different scenarios and building organizational and individual "muscle memory." When a behavior is repeated over time, a long-term memory is created for that task, eventually allowing it to be performed without conscious effort.

This is particularly true when a crisis first occurs. The assessment and activation process (Chapter 7) can be very straightforward but runs smoothly only with preparation and practice. You want your organization to have a well-defined and well-practiced incident assessment process so that problems, incidents, or potential or real crises are immediately recognized, assessed and acted upon. Having heightened risk awareness and an assessment process in place will save time in the first few moments of a crisis and make a great difference in response, recovery time and efforts.

Idea #6: Knowledge capture

How effective are your crisis plans, training and exercises? Do your training and exercises cover what someone would need to know in order to perform in a crisis? Have you captured the basics of what the team needs to do to get started in managing the crisis? A tremendous amount of critical knowledge and business information is often scattered among spreadsheets, original documents, or in the heads of a few subject matter experts. What happens when that subject matter expert (SME) goes on vacation or – yikes – if they retire? This is increasingly an issue in many companies as baby boomers leave the workforce, often taking a headful of institutional knowledge with them.

Crisis management planning is a perfect avenue to collect and organize that information for future use and to prevent the information from being lost forever. A well-crafted, all-hazards crisis plan is the first thing you need. But a plan is just a plan. What will make your teams great is practice. I am not suggesting that you have lots of crises, but you do need a solid exercise program that will challenge your most experienced team members and enhance the skills of more junior employees. During a crisis, the first reaction most people have is not to grab a plan; they tend to just start doing things. They rely on muscle memory and their experiences. Make sure that the muscle memory and experience they are relying on is what they practiced in their last great exercise.

Idea #7: Increased robustness

The crisis management planning process can strengthen the organization, not just by preparing for major disruptions, but also by giving employees the skills and knowledge to react more effectively to mitigate smaller everyday problems as they arise – and before they can become major disruptions.

Everyone knows what it's like when the most senior person, who has everything in their head, goes on vacation. People scramble frantically to make sure they know what to do if something goes wrong. Just think of the amount of increased resiliency you could create by transferring information through plans, documents, training, and exercises. Everyone's knowledge will increase, along with the company's ability to recover.

Idea #8: Deeper knowledge

When engaged in the crisis planning process and in participating in crisis exercises, we have had clients say that they actually learned even more about their current processes and how to perform them more effectively and efficiently by participating in crisis preparation. And even for veteran employees, this process can lead to deeper knowledge, which can improve day-to-day work.

It is possible to use a crisis as an opportunity for creating a better organization. This requires that our leaders develop a willingness to explore not only the strengths, but the weaknesses of the organization and themselves. Some deep soul-searching can lead to deeper personal awareness. When people are aware, they can change, learn, and grow.

> **❝ *Your brand is what people say about you when you're not in the room.* ❞**
> — **Jeff Bezos**
> Amazon founder

Communicating value

This brings us to the question of communicating the value that you are creating in your program, plans, and exercises. You need to start thinking of crisis management as a product that needs to be marketed strategically within your organization. Really.

We divide these marketing efforts into two categories: overt and covert. Overt marketing efforts are just as the word describes: they're done or shown in the open and are plainly or readily apparent to everyone. For example, you could encourage employee home preparedness during the month of September which happens to be "National Preparedness Month." To build resiliency, you need employees to show up at time of disaster, and they will only show up if their families and homes are OK. One way to make that a better possibility is to encourage home preparedness. That way your "National Preparedness Month" activities feed into a win-win for your program and the company.

Covert marketing, on the other hand, is not openly acknowledged or displayed. There are ways you can share information and knowledge, thus informing others, but can also demonstrate the value you provide. For example, if your management is keenly interested in cyberattacks and cyber preparation, it would be very appropriate (and help build your program's value) if you kept him or her informed of key attacks or responses by other similar companies or competitors. Keep them in the loop on things that they might not likely see themselves, which can reinforce the value you bring to the organization. And when appropriate, do analysis of contemporary events and share that with key individuals.

And whenever key events occur, find ways to bring the information to the right people in your organization:

- Write after-action reports for real activations or exercises. Be sure to outline the ways that the crisis process helped, the key lessons learned, and next steps.
- Refer back to your internal marketing plan. Whether you had a real activation or held a great exercise, tell your story by internal communications vehicles, such as company articles, whitepapers, and/or presentations.

Elevator speech challenge

An elevator speech is a clear, brief message or "commercial" about your program. It communicates what it is, what it does, and how it benefits the organization in a time of crisis and every day. It's typically about 30 seconds, about the time it takes people to ride from the top to the bottom of a building in an elevator.[21]

You need a great elevator speech because in this day and age, people don't have much time and you need to clearly and succinctly be able to communicate the value of the crisis management program at any time and in any place. Here's a way to get your elevator speech started:

1. Write down everything that comes up in your mind.
2. Edit, edit, edit. Make strong short and powerful sentences. Eliminate all unnecessary words.
3. Connect the key concepts and words to each other. This

---

21   "The 30 Second Elevator Speech," UC Davis, http://sfp.ucdavis.edu/files/163926. pdf

needs to flow naturally and smoothly.

4. Memorize key points.

5. Practice, practice, practice, anywhere and everywhere. Start with your bathroom mirror.

6. Remember the key question of your listener: "What's in it for me?"

Here's your challenge: Write it, practice it, deliver it. And see what it can do for your program. It will almost certainly sharpen how you talk about crisis management whether you're in the elevator or not.

Summary

When reflecting on the ways that crisis management is important to your organization, it is critical that you spend quality time to truly understand the value that it brings beyond the time of crisis. Your challenge is to find ways to always market the program's value and tout its daily contributions to the organization. Get started writing that elevator speech today!

CHAPTER 10

How to create a top-notch Crisis Management Team and program

Chapter topics
- *Executive management support for your program*
- *Business continuity management governance plan*
- *Plan and roadmap for success*

❝ *Good management is the art of making problems so interesting and their solutions so constructive that everyone wants to get to work and deal with them.* **❞**

— **Paul Hawken**
American environmentalist,
entrepreneur and author

Introduction

One of the most common concerns I hear from other crisis management and business continuity professionals is how to get senior management to take this work seriously, stay engaged and support the program both financially and with their influence. Executives often "get it" after an incident has occurred; the goal is to engage them before that happens.

Creating a solid crisis management program and team basically boils down to having three things:

- Strong executive management support
- An established business continuity management governance document
- A solid program development plan and a roadmap for execution

These critical components work in concert with each other. For your best success, ticking these off in the order above would serve you well. In particular, effective and engaged executive support, as with many other projects, is key to the success of your efforts.

Building support throughout the organization

You will have to reach across and up the organization to assure your success. That, however, is easier said than done.

Where to begin? Start with your boss – *without her or his support, things are far more difficult.* Work with your boss to map out a plan.

Start by figuring out who might be receptive thought-leaders:

- Are there any C-suite executives who have some interest in crisis management? Don't be surprised if there are none ... that's not unusual – just think of it as an opportunity.
- Are there any who see crisis management as a questionable matter or, worse, a waste of time and money? It is better to know who they are so you can change their minds down the road.
- Likewise, are there any departments or locations that have some interest in crisis management? If there are, they are a great starting point and a base from which to build support.
- And are there any who are notably dismissive of crisis management? Reframe them in your mind as opportunities for the future.

Once you have the lay of the land, you can begin to think – with your boss – about how to build understanding and support for a plan and team. Who might be a good senior management and/or executive sponsor?

Here is a word to the wise: If your boss is wise and respected up and down the organization, all of this will go reasonably well. If, on the other hand, your boss sees no need to build support, or, worse, is disdainful of networking through the company, you'll have to sort it out on your own ... with some considerable care. You will then need to cultivate contacts and supporters throughout the company and build your own network without alienating your boss.

Building strong executive management support

Once you have identified likely candidates as sponsor(s), you need to carefully think about what you want from them. Let's approach this by asking three questions:

- What do you want the executive sponsor to do?
- How do you build their support?
- What can executive management do on an on-going basis to support the program?

What do you want the executive sponsor to do?

As a joke, you may say, "Fund my program!" Well yes, funding is important, but many projects still fail when money is the only visible support given. Sometimes money is the easy part. So what, then, is the role and responsibility of your executive sponsor?[22]

1. Formally define the project, the crisis/business continuity manager, and the team
2. Champion the project team with resources and visible support
3. Defend the project and team against organizational interference

If your program lacks an executive sponsor, then the heavy lifting – including any political fallout – will likely fall on the shoulders of the crisis manager.

---

22   Petty, Art, "Five Tips to Gain Executive Support for Your Project," The Balance, October 21, 2017, https://www.thebalance.com/manager-needs-supportive-executive-sponsor-4046176

Ten ways to work with an Executive Sponsor to support your program

A crisis management project's success is dependent, to an increasing degree, not only on the efforts of the crisis manager but also on the efforts of the executive. Here are things that can be done to build support for your program. Five are for the crisis manager, five are for the executive.[23]

Crisis Manager

1. First and foremost, enlist a sponsor – the most senior person possible. Emphasize the role and responsibilities of the sponsor as identified above. Use contemporary crisis examples that connect crisis project success and effective sponsorship.

2. Educate them in the program and in ways they can offer meaningful support. You need them to support the strategic aspects of the crisis program, not the tactical. Brief them about the program, the issues, and ways they can assist in the organization.

3. Engage them in activities only when it provides value. Encourage them to kick off trainings or exercises, to provide encouragement and cheerleading to the crisis team, and to show genuine interest. They don't need to stay for the whole program – just getting them to start the day will signal to all that this is important.

---

23   Ibid page 150.

4. Ensure that the program is supported by a strong governance program:
   a) Identify any resistance to the program and determine how to best overcome objections.
   b) Support adequate budget allocation to maintain the program and meet its goals.
   c) Support program oversight by creating a Steering Committee with full authority to perform all tasks as signed to it in the Business Continuity Management policy statement of the governance document.
5. Leverage your sponsor wisely and use her or him appropriately. You need them to secure resources, serve as a spokesperson for the crisis program and be the executive face for the crisis program in the company.

Executive Sponsor

1. Act as advocate for crisis management to other executives, the board of directors, and the rest of the company.
2. Advocate for including a regular report on the overall status of crisis management and business continuity to the Board (or the appropriate Board committee).
3. Ensure that the executive management team participates in tactical crisis management team exercises, so they can better understand and practice their strategic role during an event.
4. Ensure that the executive management team has its own dedicated annual exercise, utilizing very realistic scenari-

os and exercise structures.

    a)   This helps to develop "muscle memory."

    b)   Encourage candid discussion regarding the people who are running the tactical crisis management team to ensure full executive confidence in those to whom response and recovery authority has been delegated.

5.   Remember, if the executive sponsor takes crisis management seriously, the rest of the company will, too.

The executive sponsor is critical to launching and maintaining a successful program. If the role of the sponsor is absent or vague, take it upon yourself to recruit and train your executive sponsors to support you, your team, and your organization for success.

Establishing a strong governance plan

A common flaw in many, if not most, Crisis Management Programs is that they lack the status of a major corporate program and policy – in other words, a governance document. There's nothing at all wrong about that, but the result is that usually there are no clear and hard rules for how Crisis Management is actually managed.

Thus, for a Crisis Management Program to be effective and resilient, it needs to have a proper charter – a governance document that defines authority, decision-making, and accountability and is endorsed and approved by Executive Management.

Ideally, these specifications for Crisis Management would exist in the firm's Business Continuity Management (BCM) Governance program and document. However, many companies don't have a BCM charter either – leaving these critical functions as vague intentions rather than critical functions.

That's why organizations need to be more formal and precise about the scope and responsibilities of BCM in general and Crisis Management in particular. The program needs to have an approved structure that allows for authority, decision-making and accountability and is endorsed and approved by Executive Management. This means there is:

- Internal commitment
- A defined end-state in mind, what the company wants the program to accomplish
- Identified mechanisms for maintaining the program over time

For the purpose of our discussion, we will refer to this as a BCM Governance program or document, rather than a stand-alone Crisis Management program.

There are three primary benefits to investing the time and energy in creating a Business Continuity Management Governance document:

1. Creates an *internal commitment*, to overcome the inertia that often prevents 'overhead' programs from developing
2. Defines the *end-state*, to establish the size, scope, and structure of the Business Continuity program
3. Specifies the *mechanisms for maintaining the program over time*, to ensure that the capability, once built, remains viable and current

The following topics should be included in a Governance Document:

- Program policy
- Program goals
- Program scope
- Program roles and responsibilities:
  - Executive management
  - Steering committee
  - Program sponsor
  - Program manager
- Program authorities:
  - Executive management
  - Steering committee
  - Program sponsor
  - Program manager
- Program review and validation:
  - Management reviews
  - Monitor and measure
  - Exercises and training
  - Continuous improvement
- Program planning:
  - Risk assessment
  - Business impact analysis
  - Business unit recovery strategies
- Operations:
  - Crisis management
  - Crisis communications

- ○ Business continuity
- ○ Technology disaster recovery
- ○ Emergency response

To build a strong governance program, you need to start by securing an executive sponsor. It's a pivotal role; consider your decision seriously. Don't be reluctant to reach high in the organization with your manager's support. Work with your sponsor to create a steering committee and select its members. (Ideally your sponsor will endorse the members and assist with bringing them on board.) Next, bring the steering committee together to "whiteboard" the major sections of the document as noted above. Then develop, review, refine, and repeat. Just like anything else in this work, it is an iterative process and will improve over time.

Building a solid plan and a roadmap for success

Great! You have the sponsor and have completed the development of the governance program and document. Congratulations, you're further ahead of the game than most! You're almost there!

Your next big task is to prepare a development plan and figure out a roadmap for program development and execution. Having a solid program and team can be achieved in about nine months, if everything is running on all cylinders.

The roadmap has five key phases:

- Phase I: Develop the Crisis Management Team Program (month one)
- Phase II: Develop the Crisis Management Plan (month two)

- Phase III: Hold a Crisis Management Team workshop (month three)
- Phase IV: Hold a Basic Tabletop exercise (month six)
- Phase V: Hold an Advanced Tabletop exercise (month nine)

Phase I – Developing the Crisis Management Team program

In this first phase, it's important to begin by developing the roadmap for an overall crisis management program for the entire organization as detailed in Chapter 5. There are two deliverables for this phase:

- Coming up with the program roadmap and roll-out strategy
- Drafting the initial Crisis Management organization charts (strategic and tactical teams) for the corporate office (which would also be used as a model for other locations)

Phase II – Developing crisis management plans

Now that you know what the world looks like, you can progress to the second phase and develop two critical documents – the strategic and tactical crisis management team plans as reviewed in Chapter 14. These should be highly actionable plans, giving the reader a high level overview of incident assessment process, roles and responsibilities of all of the players, incident action planning, command center organization and interactions with other locations.

- Develop Executive Crisis Management Plan

- Develop Crisis Management Plan for tactical team

Phase III – Holding a Crisis Management Team workshop

Once you have developed the crisis management structure and the written plans, it is critical that all the players be trained in the process, the entire company structure, incident assessment and their roles and responsibility. The workshop should also include an orientation-style exercise because adults learn by doing, not by sitting and listening to presentations.

So, after you have reviewed the didactic material with them, you must get them engaged by conducting an orientation exercise[24]. This type of exercise has a simple narrative and allows the participants to assume their crisis role, look through the newly-created plan, and figure out what they would do. At this point in the workshop, people get a much better feel for their role during a crisis.

Your workshop should be about four hours, which would include an orientation exercise with a contextualized scenario. And don't forget to gather feedback from your team members and write up a workshop and exercise after-action report!

Phase IV – Holding a basic tabletop exercise for the Crisis Management Team

This phase really starts to get into developing the team's mus-

---

24   Phelps, Regina, Emergency Management Exercises: From Response to Recovery, Chandi Media, December 2010, page, 143. https://tinyurl.com/y73ox597

cle memory. In this phase, you should hold a Tabletop exercise that lasts three or four hours[25]. This basic tabletop exercise will help get them further into their roles and responsibilities. Importantly, it also has them working with their team members to craft responses to a variety of challenges.

In a Tabletop exercise, you start with a baseline narrative and then have the story progress. This is done via the introduction of exercise injects, which are additional issues, problems, or incidents that the team has to resolve. Just like in the real world, the crisis situation always changes, and additional problems crop up. After learning the baseline story, the teams start to receive injects which cause them to refer to their plans, talk to their colleagues, and decide what they would do next to solve the problem.

In this phase, you'll develop the Tabletop exercise, and then conduct it. And again, don't forget to develop the exercise after-action report.[26]

Phase V – Holding an advanced tabletop exercise for the Crisis Management Team

Phase V is where you'll develop a much more hands-on and realistic exercise. The goal at this point is to provide the team with an opportunity to go even deeper into their crisis team knowledge and learning. An Advanced Tabletop[27] is one that is fully simulated. In

---

25   Ibid Emergency Management Excercises, Chandi Media, Regina Phelps, December 2010

26   Ibid page 193.

27   Ibid page 164.

66 *The ratio of We's to I's is the best indicator of the development of a team.* **99**

— **Lewis B. Ergen**
American actor

this kind of exercise, instead of the exercise players simply *saying* what they would do (as they do in a Basic Tabletop), they need to go talk to someone about their problem or issue. This is done because it makes the team look closer into their plans and get realistic feedback on their responses.

What is the difference between a Basic Tabletop versus an Advanced Tabletop? In a basic tabletop, the players just talk about what they would do. I call this a "blah, blah, blah" exercise. It is a helpful and important part of their training (especially with a new team or revised plan), but to truly deepen someone's learning, they need to have a more *experiential* exercise where team members have to speak to someone to resolve their issue. When approached, a Simulation Team member will 'magically' turn into the person the exercise player needs them to be, "the caller" of an inject. After listening to the team member's response, the Simulator may love the answer, may hate it, may have lots of questions, or may even push back. This is all great for the exercise player, because it teaches new skills, builds deeper knowledge, and helps to develop that muscle memory. It's also a lot of fun!

Your Phase V tasks are to develop the Advanced Tabletop exercise, and then conduct it. And again, don't forget to develop the exercise after-action report.

Summary

The three steps contained in this chapter are critical to the success of developing a solid crisis management program. Although this is chapter ten, it is likely where your journey really begins. You need the executive support, the governance document, and the roadmap to be able to create the plan that your organization requires, your employees need, and your customers and clients demand.

THREE

Crisis process

> **66** *Organizing is what you do*
> *before you do something*
> *so that when you do it,*
> *it is not all mixed up.* **99**

— **A. A. Milne**
Author of *Winnie the Pooh*

Congratulations...you have done a lot of work to get to this point. You have identified:

- Who is on the team(s)
- What your structure is
- When to activate
- Where to convene
- Why this work is important
- How to create a great team and program

The good news, is that you've accomplished a lot! The bad

news is that even after you've done the 5W's and an H, you still have plenty of work to do.

Now we need to look at the crisis processes you must have in place so your team can hit the ground running – five critical areas that need your attention:

- Situational awareness
- Incident action planning
- Department Operations Centers (DOC)
- Crisis Management Team (CMT) plans
- Sustained operations

CHAPTER 11

What is *Situational Awareness* and why do you need it?

Chapter topics
- *OODA loop*
- *Collect, validate and assess information*
- *Information management display*

> **❝***An organization's ability to learn, and translate that learning into action rapidly, is the ultimate competitive advantage.***❞**
> — **Jack Welch**
> American businessman

Introduction

Situational Awareness is the ability to identify, process, and comprehend the critical elements of information regarding an incident. Simply said, it's *knowing what is going on around you.* Another term used by the military is *Common Operational Picture* which is defined as a single identical display of relevant (operational) information (e.g. position of your own troops and enemy troops, etc.) shared by more than one Command[28]. Same thing, just different words.

When we fail to have a good understanding of the incident – inadequate situational awareness – poor decision making, inadequate communications and weak management of the crisis is likely to follow. It sounds easy in principle, but in reality, it requires a process, tools and practices. This is overlooked by many Crisis Management Team and Emergency Operations Centers (EOC) and results in scrambling at the last moment to figure out the information management process and fully understand the incident and its impacts.

Situational awareness has two distinct activities
- Collect: Observe, acquire and compile the information
- Process: Assess the information and orient yourself to the possible impacts

Once you have the situational awareness, you can make the necessary decisions and then act.

John Boyd and the OODA Loop

Colonel John Boyd was a remarkable individual in American military history. A great U.S. fighter pilot, considered by some to be the father of the F-15, F-16 F-18 and an influential military theorist. His manual of fighter tactics changed the way every air force in the world flies and fights. During his time at the Weapons

---

28   Common operational picture, https://en.wikipedia.org/wiki/Common_operational_picture

School, he developed his OODA (observe, orient, decide, and act) concept – a decision-making process that every individual can use. Boyd instructed pilots that the one who can cycle through their OODA process loop quicker than their opponent during combat would gain the tactical advantage. The OODA Loop enabled pilots to adapt quickly to rapidly changing situations. The OODA loop requires situational awareness – just like what your crisis management team needs.

OODA Loop

The OODA Loop was Colonel Boyd's way of explaining how we go through the process of reacting to stimuli.

- **Observe** – While approximately 80% of the information we receive comes from our sense of sight, we can and do make observations with our other senses. For instance, you might hear a gunshot and not see the person who fired it.
- **Orient** – Once you look and see the source of the gunfire, you are now orienting yourself. You are now focusing your attention on what you have just observed.
- **Decide** – You have to make a decision on what to do about what you have just observed and what caused you to focus your attention on the incident.
- **Act** – Once you have made a decision, you now need to do something.

The OODA loop is what happens between the onset of a stimulus and the onset of a reaction to that stimulus. Gathering situational awareness is both the observe and orient step in the OODA loop.

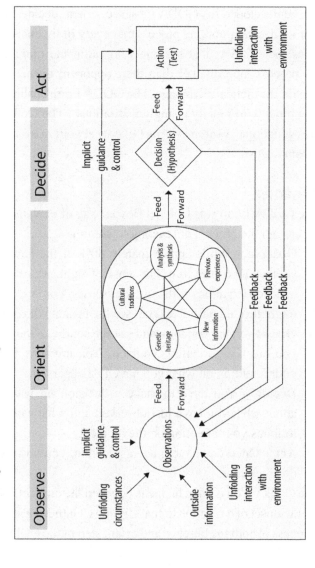

Schematic of the OODA loop via Wikipedia

Drinking out of a fire hose

Crisis Management teams sometimes say that managing the information during a crisis is like drinking out of a fire hose. How does one do that? Carefully and hopefully with a plan that has been thought out and practiced in advance. These are some of the questions you need to think about:

- What are your information sources, where do you find them and do you trust them?
- How do you assess the information?
- How can you validate the information?
- How do you display it in a meaningful way so that decision-makers can take in the information, make decisions and then act?

Collect information – Easier said than done

Information is critical in a crisis. To gauge and act on the situation, we must 1) collect and 2) process the data quickly and unerringly. The problem is knowing what is critical, what is nominal, and what is simply wrong. Crisis management teams can be easily overwhelmed by the volume of data or, worse, misled by false and irrelevant information. The first task is to get the information – data collection. Data collection is the process of gathering and measuring information in an established systematic fashion.

Let's start by considering the sources and how to acquire the information.

Information sources

Where is your information coming from? It may feel like it is coming from everywhere but there are generally two sources: internal and external.

Internal information

Internal information is available only to the business and is from within the business. There are two types of information sources within organizations: formal and informal.

Formal

Formal information sources are well-established groups with a clear mission. A classic example in a company is command or operations centers. Many organizations have 24-hour command centers for a variety of different functions:

- Security Operations Centers (SOC)
- Network Operations Centers (NOC)
- Supply Chain Monitoring

Additionally, there might also be:

- Customer Service Centers and hotlines servicing your customers
- Employee Hotlines receiving information, often confidentially, from employees
- Claims Centers
- Vendors and contractors (this can also include vendor monitoring of systems)

These formal sources usually have an internal reporting mechanism within their own department or group, but how does that information get shared with the Incident Assessment or Crisis Management Teams? I call these localized departments or groups "feeders." If a company hasn't figured out how to get the information from these discrete "feeder" groups, then you have a big problem. How do you know what is going on in a timely manner, so you can respond appropriately and in a timely fashion?

Map out the formal functions, teams and processes within your organization and then ask yourself – "how does this information come to us at time of crisis?" Then you need to formalize this intake process, so it is automatic as possible.

Informal

Informal communication – the so-called "grapevine" – has no structure and obeys no rules. It can be well-intended or not. It can be accurate or not. It might come from conversations, electronic mails, text messages or phone calls between socializing employees. The obvious risk is that false information can spread stunningly fast and create all kinds of difficulties, even danger. Your leaders and the communications people need to communicate quickly, clearly and accurately about what's going on. Failure to do that just heats up the rumor mill and erodes credibility when credibility is crucial.

All incoming *internal* information – whether received formally or informally – needs to be quickly but thoroughly checked and validated. And, in general, shared as soon as possible with all those affected and involved. This process – intake, validation, and

necessary communications back out – is one of the key responsibilities of the Planning and/or Communications team in the EOC.
Failure to do it well may involve the safety of people and will be
remembered long after the event.

External information

External information comes from third parties *outside* your
organization. It can range from the guidance by local emergency
services or federal agencies to web posts by your own employees,
subject experts, kibitzers and kooks.

Primary sources

The most likely and trustworthy outside sources are typically
from the public service sector. Depending on the crisis you are dealing with, their information and/or advice could be quite valuable:

Local police, fire and emergency medical services (EMS)

Federal government agencies such as FBI, Department of
Homeland Security (DHS), United States Cyber Command . . .
and the National Weather Service (or comparable agencies if your
crisis is in another country)

- State Office of Emergency Services (OES)
- County OES
- Global risk data providers
- Geographic information systems (GIS) modeling
- Global medical information
- Real-time employee travel data

These sources tend to be reliable, but they are not infallible.

And some of them are sometimes slow to respond. In any case, try to fact-check or triangulate whatever they may be reporting or advising.

Secondary sources

Other outside sources of information range from potentially very helpful to hard-to-verify or flat-out misleading.

News sites (e.g. *New York Times, Washington Post, Wall Street Journal* . . . local/regional newspapers, radio and TV)

Social media (e.g. Facebook, Twitter, LinkedIn, Instagram) . . . with helpful comments, disparaging remarks, or sometimes simply false statements

- Chat rooms that follow your industry
- Blogs (e.g. Brian Krebs for information/cyber security)
- Websites that review organizations (e.g. Glassdoor)
- Sites that specifically follow your organization or business sector

In the heat of a crisis, it's hard to monitor all such outlets, but it would be wise to task someone to keep an eye on Facebook and Twitter at a minimum. While there could be a lot of inconsequential comments or worse, it's conceivable that employees might text messages for help (if they are trapped or injured) or other important information. There are a variety of social media monitoring tools that your communications team may already use on a daily basis.

Spot-check the other sites and report any posts that provide any new insights into what's going on or, more likely, comments that are misleading, erroneous, or flat-out malicious. The latter need to be countered as quickly as possible by your Communication team with the advice and consent of the Incident Commander.

> **❝ *It's not information overload.*
> *It's filter failure.* ❞**
>
> — Clay Shirky
> Consultant and author

Once you have identified all of the sources – internal and external – you now need to "aim" the information at the internal target within your EOC who will do the validation and assessment. If the information comes from an existing command or call centers, they must be informed that the Crisis Management Team has activated and where to forward information. If it is from the departments who monitor external sources and sites, they need to be informed of the activation, what information you are looking for (key words, phrases and if necessary, more detail on the incident) and how to forward it to the right party in the EOC.

Now that you have it – Now what? Validate, assess, display

So now you have information coming into your command center from multiple internal and external sources. How do you validate, assess and display it in a way that provides meaningful information to the entire team and to leadership for decision-making? This is no easy task.

Information management the old-fashioned way

The old-fashioned way is teams of people reviewing the information and manually inputting information to be displayed. The vast majority of EOCs operate in this fashion.

Validate

This is where the fire hose metaphor really comes into play. Take a moment to look at the information sources we have just reviewed. Stop and really think about them. Once you have received data from them, who in the EOC assesses and validates the information? It is usually the Planning and/or Communications teams. Pull together your teams and whiteboard this process – literally – walking through the steps to understand how it will play out.

Much of what you read and hear about is from online sources. Your radio and television news are also fed by the internet. As we know from the amount of made up information and bogus stories, we need to be careful when consuming our news. What are your current strategies for assessing the information for accuracy? *LibrarySource* provides some good tips on how to assess the validity and trustworthiness of online information[29]:

---

29 Spotting fake news and validating information, The librarian's role in verifying trust
    and reliability, https://libsource.com/spotting-fake-news/

- Obtain your news and information from trusted sources you know are reliable, rather than just social media networks.
- Always look for a least two sources for any story.
- Check the URL and note the domain address of the webpage – in particular the extension – the two or three letters that follow the dot. Most extensions can be acquired by anyone. Certain ones – like .edu for education and .gov for government – are restricted.
- Identify who is behind any suspect website by using a "who is" lookup service[30]. This gives you more information about the site and possibly who is behind it.
- Assess the writing style – academic or journalism style will include concrete details that can be verified, rather than language that is vague or purely editorial. Citations and attributions will be included and backed with links to legitimate sources.
- Look for an About Us page, which will be missing or vague on a suspect website. A legitimate About Us page will confirm credentials and help identify biases and agendas.
- Use fact-checking sites like FactCheck.org[31], which is a project of the University of Pennsylvania's Annenberg Public Policy Center.
- Look for an author or publisher name and date of publication.

---

30   ICANNWHOIS, https://whois.icann.org/en
31   University of Pennsylvania's Annenberg Public Policy Center

- Check multiple sources for different points of view.

Assess and prioritize

Once you have validated the information, you need to assess and prioritize it. In a crisis, you are likely to have a lot of information flowing into the EOC. Not everything is important. If you only got one piece of information, it could be ranked "critical" but what if you have two, ten, 200, 500 or more discrete data points?

Who prioritizes the information into helpful categories, so the most critical information rises to the top? Most organizations have three levels:

- Critical (red)
- Important (yellow)
- General (green)

Color coding or different fonts (bold, italics, underline) may help for immediate recognition.

When critical information is received, how do you let everyone know immediately? It could be as simple as a verbal announcement in the EOC, a text message or email. This is really important – if everyone has a slightly different view of the crisis – your decisions will reflect a disjointed response.

Display

Once it has been validated and assessed, it needs to be packaged in a way that the information is available and useable. Is that on flipcharts, whiteboards or electronic status boards? You need the following types of status boards:

- **General status** – this holds the "basic facts" of the incident and is an historical timeline of the incident.
- **Regional status** – for regional events with widespread impacts such as an earthquake or hurricane, you need to know the status of the critical infrastructure of your area – not just for your business but to understand the impact to your employee and customers as well. This could include the status of roads, bridges, airports, public transportation, schools, hospitals, utilities, communication services and information sources (TV, radio, internet).
- **Critical incident decisions** – Decisions that are important and that everyone needs to know. Examples include: Office closed till next Monday. All employees will be paid through the week. Employees must report availability to managers.
- **News status** – listing of stories about the incident, your organization's talking points and responses.
- **Team status boards** – each team needs to keep a status board of the critical issues in their area, their objectives and status.
- **Technology dashboard** – Because technology affects everyone and their ability to do their job, a simple dashboard noting the status of key aspects of the technology is helpful. This may include data centers, network, Voice Over Internet Protocol (VOIP) and key applications.

If you are using project management software, you could use the same status boards as noted above or on different topics. They could be in the team's area or pushed to all team members.

Validate, assess, prioritize and display in one package

Many organizations are drowning in data on a routine day which means they are underwater at the time of a crisis. There are some technology companies that are developing products to help with managing the information for more efficient decision-making.

❝ *Information overload will lead to 'future shock syndrome' as an individual will suffer severe physical and mental disturbances.* **❞**

— Alvin Toffler,
Author – Future Shock

Information Management in the data age

Critical Event Management (CEM)

Everbridge[32] (www.everbridge.com) has recently released a product called *Critical Event Management (CEM)* which looks at

---

32 Full disclosure – I occasionally do speaking and writing engagements for Everbridge.

the organization's critical assets (people, facilities, supply chain, IT and reputation and brand) and the intersection of risk (internal and external). Their product helps manage the information of those critical events by assessing over 100+ data sources using data analytics. This ties to their emergency notification system tool for ease in prompt communication.

CEM can be engineered to support a variety of activities, including the ability to assess, locate, act, analyze, visualize, orchestrate, communicate, and collaborate. Because of these skills, CEM can be used to gather information and rapidly and effectively respond to any type of crisis including severe weather, workplace violence, terrorism, cyber-attack, IT incidents and managing supply chain disruptions.

At the time of the crisis, CEM has the ability to align all the resources necessary to manage the organization's response to the event and can enable communication alerts to identified key stakeholders. These stakeholders could include executive management, crisis management teams, security, facilities, IT, environmental health, safety professionals and customer support, as well as external partners such as supply chain partners or emergency responders.

To find Everbridge and other possible vendors, search online for "virtual command centers" or "threat assessment and operational visualization software."

Other virtual options

If you are using an EOC software or a project management software in your EOC, they can be used to display and share information although the inputs to them will be manual. Some of our clients have taken their existing monitoring tools and using homemade widgets, created a monitoring tool to bring some of the information together. These homemade solutions can be helpful but usually require manual assistance.

Summary

Situational awareness is essential for managing an incident. Your crisis management team needs good, solid information to protect employees, make decisions, communicate and ultimately restore the business. Pull together a group to work through this issue now so you can launch it immediately at the time of a crisis.

CHAPTER 12

Incident Action Plans – Roadmaps for success

Chapter topics
- *Planning P*
- *SMART objectives*
- *Incident Action Plan meetings*

❝ *Action expresses priorities.* **❞**
— Mahatma Gandhiand

Introduction

When you plan a long driving vacation, you probably think about a number of things – where are we going, how long will it take, what will it take to make it a success, what do we have to do before we leave? You need to answer those same kinds of questions to develop an Incident Action Plan (IAP).

An Incident Action Plan is the hallmark of the Incident Command System (ICS). I believe that a well-developed IAP is a critical tool for any crisis – regardless of whether you use ICS or not.

It's just smart management.

Incident Action Plans

An IAP formally documents incident objectives, operational period objectives, and the response strategy as defined by crisis leadership during response planning. It contains general tactics to achieve goals and objectives within the overall strategy while providing important information on incident and response parameters.[33] The incident action planning process requires collaboration and participation among all crisis management leaders and their teams.

The incident action planning process is built on the following five phases:

1. Situational awareness – understand the situation
2. Objectives – establish incident objectives
3. Prepare – prepare the plan
4. Communicate – disseminate the plan
5. Repeat – execute, evaluate, and revise the plan

Planning P

The Planning "P" is a brilliant picture of all of the stages in the incident action planning process. Developed by the U.S. Coast Guard, it is a great visual tool to teach IAP development and helps keep your team on track during an activation and as the planning

---

33   Incident Action Plans, U.S. Department of Health & Humans Services, Public Health Emergencies, What is an Incident Action Plan? https://www.phe.gov/Preparedness/planning/mscc/handbook/Pages/appendixc.aspx

process gets started.

The leg of the "P" *(flowchart on next page)* includes the initial steps of awareness, assessment and activation:

- Incident occurs
- Gain situational awareness
- Assess the incident – Incident Assessment Team assess the incident
- Decision – Activate (or not)
- Notify – Executives, Crisis Management Team (CMT) and Department Operational Centers (DOCs)
- Brief – Conduct short initial briefings with Executives, CMT and DOCs

Once the initial assessment and declaration processes have been completed, we move into the "loop section" of the P. As the word loop implies, you do this over and over again until the incident has resolved. Although maintaining situational awareness is essential throughout the life cycle of the incident, the steps in Phase 1 of the Planning P are done only once.

Once Phase 1 is accomplished, crisis management then shifts into a cycle of planning and operations, informed by ongoing situational awareness and is repeated for each operational period. This loop becomes the Operations "O" of the letter P.

Operational period

An operational period is the period of time scheduled for performing a given set of operational objectives as specified in the IAP. The length of the operational period can be quite short at the

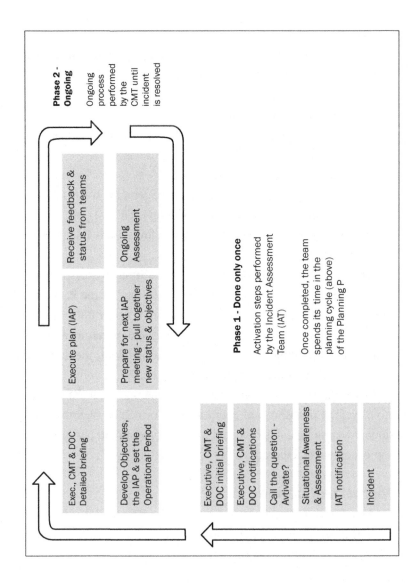

beginning – two to four hours at the beginning of the incident requiring extensive response efforts. Operational periods are subsequently reviewed and adjusted throughout the life cycle of the incident as operations require, adjusting to typically 8, 12 or 24 hours as the crisis evolves.

Situational awareness

Initial situational awareness involves understanding the situation and establishing initial incident priorities. As noted in the previous chapter, gaining an understanding of the situation includes gathering, validating, assessing and displaying information regarding the scale, scope, complexity, and potential incident impacts. Comprehensive situational awareness is essential to developing and implementing an effective IAP.

Once you have the basic initial situational awareness, then the initial priorities can be developed. Clear and specific initial priorities are important to establishing direction early in the crisis response process. When the members of the CMT clearly understand the resolve and commitment behind objectives, they are better equipped to act decisively and make better decisions. With many things vying for your attention, not everything can be a priority. The initial priority list helps to keep the team focused and grounded on what is agreed upon as the important priorities.

A very common set of initial incident priorities may include:

- Life safety – ensure the safety of employees, contractor responders in the recovery effort
- Incident stabilization – prevent the situation from getting

worse
- Property and equipment preservation – mitigate where possible and preserve company property and equipment
- Return to business as usual – get back to "business-as-usual" as quickly as possible

Objectives

Who develops the IAP objectives? These are developed by each of the teams and presented at an IAP meeting by the team leader (sometimes called a section chief) of the individual teams in the CMT. For the initial IAP, the team leaders huddle with their teams to determine the initial objectives, and the objectives are presented at the IAP meeting by the team leaders.

Incident objectives:
- Drive response and recovery activities
- Utilize realistic expectations of what can be accomplished when resources have been effectively applied
- Must be flexible enough to allow for a variety of solutions
- Set guidance and direction, but do not specify tactics
- Answer the question of what must be accomplished and when

Qualities of a "good' objective

A well-written – SMART -- objective has the following qualities:
- S – Specific
- M – Measurable

- A – Achievable
- R – Relevant and Realistic
- T – Timely
- They:
  - are short, clear and concise
  - always start with an action-oriented verb
  - bring structure and trackability into your objectives
  - create verifiable trajectories toward a certain objective, with clear milestones and an estimation of the goal's attainability

Each objective must be assigned to a person within the team. This shows accountability and identifies who can be contacted if there are questions about the objectives going forward.

Examples of a "good' objective

The following are examples of IAP objectives by team:

Human Resources
- Account for all employees
- Determine need for employee assistance program counseling services
- Notify injured employees emergency contact of an incident and the employees condition and location

Operations (Corporate Infrastructure)
- Conduct an initial building damage assessment
- Contact contractors for emergency repairs
- Appoint a liaison to work with emergency responders

Technology
- Conduct an initial technology assessment including infra-structure, applications and network
- Assess physical assets
- Reroute company main number to alternate site

Planning (Business Operations)
- Assess impact to time-sensitive business processes
- Activate affected business continuity plans as necessary
- Determine the immediate work-arounds and what should be instituted in priority order

Communications
- Communicate company status with key stakeholders using approved talking points (list all stakeholders here)
- Update company website
- Update employee hotline

Finance
- Issue a disaster accounting code to the CMT to account for all crisis expenses
- Contact all appropriate insurance carriers
- Document all physical damage with video or still images

Prepare

Once the teams have prepared their objectives, the Incident Commander and team leaders meet to review status and share objectives. This meeting is run with precision and is meant to be short, disciplined and concise. Meetings should be less than 30 minutes – ideally between 15 – 25 minutes. The Incident Commander leads the meeting and an appointed scribe (usually from the Command team) records the information.

IAP Agenda (physical or virtual)

- Roll call of all participants
- Brief description of the meeting agenda
  - New situational awareness or status updates
  - Team leaders report on any status updates on objectives
  - Team leaders share new objectives
  - Missing anything?
- The Incident Commander first acts for any new situational awareness or overall status updates from the assembled team leaders
- Team leaders then report status on objectives, specific issues, needs or requests
- Team leaders share new objectives
- Incident Commander asks if anything is missing
- New operational period is determined

When team leaders are preparing to attend the IAP meeting they must have:

- Status of the incident from the perspective of the team
- Status on your team's assigned objectives
- New proposed objectives
- Plan to execute the objectives and any necessary requirements (tools, equipment) to achieve the objectives

In order for the IAP meetings to be as productive as possible, meeting rules should be very clear. Agreed upon meeting rules should be reviewed before every meeting to keep everyone on point.

- Only invitees speak; others who may attend do so with permission and are not speakers
- No mobile phones used during the meeting
- No sidebar conversations
- No interruptions unless an emergency
- Have the IAP meeting in a quiet room away from distractions

Some of our clients run the meetings with everyone standing. Turns out that people run more efficient meetings when people are on their feet and there is no time wasted. If you want to try that, circle your team and have the scribe list status first and then objectives on a flip chart. Everyone can view the written plan and make changes or suggestions in real time.

Lastly, in some events, the Incident Commander may set information thresholds and the team leaders must report based on those thresholds. For example, the Incident Commander may call for "exception reporting" only. These are instances in which actual performance deviated significantly from expectations and usually in a negative direction. The intent of this type of report is to focus attention on just those areas requiring immediate action and perhaps additional resources or assistance. If there are no exceptions to report, the Incident Commander assumes that all work is going according to plan.

Disseminate

Once the meeting concludes, the IAP is developed and written. This always follows the same format:

- Situation status
- Objectives (by team) with named assignments
- Operational period
- Any additional documents such as news releases, talking points, press coverage or other pertinent information

The IAP can be written by the Command team, often the Command support team or the Planning team. Once it is completed it can be shared to the Executives, CMT, DOCs, other company locations and any key stakeholders who need to see what is happening in the management of the incident. It should be turned into a PDF document before sharing and then sent out via the usual communication channels.

If something unexpected occurs in the middle of the opertional period or something happens that everyone must know about or that will likely change the response, the team leaders are called back for a status update and the IAP may be revised to meet the new developments. The process is flexible and adjusts as the situation shifts and changes.

Repeat

Once you get into the loop of the Planning P, the team stays in that planning loop until the incident resolves. As the time passes, the operational periods become longer – often reaching a 24-hour cycle.

❝A common characteristic of people who accomplish something unusual is their understanding of, and focus on, the objective. If you get the objectives right, a lieutenant can write the strategy.❞

— **General George Marshall**
Secretary of State and Defense
under President Harry Truman

Summary

A well-written IAP organizes the CMT into a well-oiled machine. It reviews what is going on, what needs to be done and when the next reporting cycle will happen – essentially everything the team needs to manage the crisis.

CHAPTER 13

Department Operations Centers (DOC) – You just might need these

Chapter topics
- *Department Operations Centers (DOC) goals and responsibilities*
- *DOC membership and relationship to the CMT*
- *DOC IAP development*

❝Alone we can do so little, together we can do so much.❞
— **Helen Keller**
American author, political activist

Introduction

What are Department Operations Centers (DOC) and do you need them? A DOC is established and activated by individual departments to coordinate and control actions specific to that department during an incident. A DOC is a physical facility or location similar to the company's Emergency Operations Center (EOC).

Departments that are response oriented likely already have a DOC although they may not call it that. Security, Facilities and Technology departments very commonly have a DOC to manage and coordinate events specific to that department. It is not uncommon for these departments to activate their DOC to manage an incident even though the company Crisis Management Team or EOC has not yet responded.

Do you need DOCs?

Maybe. As noted above, response-type departments (Security, Facilities and IT) are a logical choice for DOCs, but others might benefit from them as well. For larger organizations (2500 employees or more), it might allow for more effective communications and management of the incident in the department. The real work of the recovery is then happening at the department level, allowing status and needs to be reported up to the CMT in the EOC for collection, coordination and centralized decision-making.

My suggestion is that you read through this chapter and at the end ask yourself the question again… "could a DOC make our crisis response process more effective?"

DOC basics

Goals and responsibilities

The goals of a DOC include:
- Extend crisis response leadership presence to the depart-

ments so response and recovery actions are being actively managed within each department

- Serve as an information collection point, to ensure that all department-specific information related to an incident is collected, consolidated and disseminated as efficiently as possible
- Serve as a coordination and communications nexus between disparate departmental functions and the Crisis Management Team (CMT).

The responsibilities of a DOC during an incident are:
- Activate when the CMT issues a directive to do so
- Receive the CMT's initial Incident Action Plan and translate all response and recovery objectives that fall within the DOC's functional scope into detailed and prioritized tactical objectives
- Mobilize and direct department resources to accomplish those tactical objectives
- Collect and consolidate information relevant to the response and recovery effort
- Inform the CMT of any logistical support or needs the DOC has in order to complete its designated activities
- Prepare and submit a DOC IAP within the timeframes defined by the CMT-defined Operational Period
- Act as a communications hub within the incident management framework.

Relationship of the DOC to the CMT

DOC Leaders should execute their responsibilities within the overall context of CMT established procedures, goals, and activity timelines. While the DOCs are accountable for ensuring that all response and recovery objectives pertinent to their departments are executed, they are also responsible for ensuring that those activities are synchronized with the overall direction established by the Incident Commander.

Relationship of the DOC to other DOCs

It is fully expected that DOC Leaders will freely communicate with each other during the course of an incident when that is the most efficient path toward meeting an operational requirement. Further, a summary of all intra-DOC communications should be included in the DOC IAP when they are relevant to the response

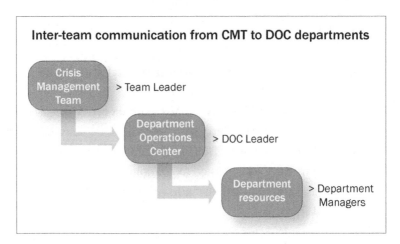

Inter-team communication from CMT to DOC departments

Crisis Management Team   > Team Leader

Department Operations Center   > DOC Leader

Department resources   > Department Managers

and recovery effort.

How is the DOC structured?

If you are using the Incident Command System with the CMT, you should use it in the DOC. Some positions (e.g. DOC Leader) are mandatory, while others are optional. The key to the organizational structure that you adopt for your DOC is to recognize that all required DOC functions must be addressed; the difference is how you allocate responsibility for those functions among various team members.

DOC Leader (Mandatory)

Responsibilities

Every DOC must have a DOC Leader, plus at least one alternate to the position. The DOC Leader is responsible for all activities that take place within the DOC, including:

- Ensuring the DOC is activated promptly when notified that an incident has occurred and addresses all response/ recovery objectives produced by the CMT
- Collecting and consolidating departmental information pertinent to the response/recovery effort
- Producing DOC IAPs and delivering them to the CMT within specified timeframes

Competencies

The DOC Leader must have deep knowledge of the department's business functions and must also possess the leadership skills to direct DOC activities with decisiveness and poise.

❝ *None of us is as smart as all of us.* ❞
— **Ken Blanchard**
Author and management expert

Position activities

- Acts as the primary liaison to the CMT
- Launches the DOC promptly upon notification
- Activates the departmental Business Continuity Plans and notifies the DOC Planning Leader
- Assumes responsibility for restoring the department's business activity (at primary or alternate location)
- Coordinates support and resources to the department
- Ensures that the DOC is adequately staffed to perform its functions and fulfill its objectives
- Determines the department's tactical response and recovery objectives
- Ensures planning meetings are conducted when required
- Supervises creation of the DOC IAP through the DOC Incident Action Plan procedure
- Coordinates with key people and officials within scope of

authority
- Informs the CMT of any necessary logistical needs
- Submits requests for additional resources to the CMT Section Chief

Planning / Business Operations Leader (Mandatory)

Responsibilities

The DOC Planning function drives the information gathering and status reporting functions of the DOC and manages execution of the departmental Business Continuity Plan when its execution has been directed.

It should be noted that the DOC Planning team may consist of the team leader and as many additional team members as are necessary to support the DOC function. The number of additional team members will be driven by multiple factors, foremost of which will likely be the department's functional complexity. For example, in the Technology DOC, the Planning section may include persons knowledgeable about networks, servers, and applications, to ensure that appropriate subject matter expertise is present in the Planning section for information gathering and status reporting purposes.

In addition, the Planning Leader must ensure that he/she provides for adequate staffing to support all data gathering and reporting responsibilities, as documented in the following sections. This support may take the form of a formally designated "Admin

Section" within the Planning team if doing so will assist in managing the anticipated workload.

The DOC Planning Leader is responsible for:

- Supporting execution of the departmental Business Continuity Plan
- Gathering and consolidating information from all available sources, both internal and external, for use during DOC IAP meetings
- Participating in DOC IAP meetings
- Disseminating incident-related information within the DOC and to department resources

Competencies

Planning Team members must have deep knowledge of the department's business functions and must be thoroughly familiar with the department's Business Impact Analysis (BIA) results.

Position activities

- Contacts department business leaders and reviews recovery time objectives, special concerns and time issues, and determines a course of action following activation of department Business Continuity Plans
- Provides assistance as necessary to ensure proper execution of the Business Continuity Plan when it has been activated
- Assists in developing departmental tactical objectives
- Provides a forum (e.g. a recurring conference call) to enable

the department to have a chance to articulate critical needs
- Consolidates all incident-related information received from the department and other sources
- Develops alternative department recovery strategies, including contingency plans that extend beyond the immediate situation
- Participates in DOC briefings and planning sessions, including DOC IAP meetings
- Keeps the DOC Leader informed of significant business events

Human Resource and Finance (Optional)

Responsibilities

The Human Resources and Finance position is primarily concerned with people-related problems including, but not limited to, employees who are injured or missing, family issues (e.g. children in school or elder care concerns), transportation and/or housing issues, employee benefits concerns, and the like.

The DOC Leader may, at his/her discretion, assign a dedicated person within the DOC to coordinate this category of questions or, alternatively, assign the responsibility to one of the existing DOC team positions.

Competencies

Human Resources and Finance Team members must have solid knowledge of the department business functions and must be capable of organizing and executing multiple tasks concurrently.

Position activities

- Coordinates DOC-specific logistic requirements with the CMT Human Resources team
- Determines immediate and ongoing DOC-specific requirements for:
  - Catering
  - Lodging
  - Transportation
- Identifies any recovery team members within the department who need immediate transportation to alternate recovery site(s)
- Works with the CMT to obtain necessary financial support (e.g. cash, increased limits on bank credit cards, emergency purchase orders or other financial and logistical support)
- Attends and participates in DOC IAP meetings

Communications (Optional)

Responsibilities

Within the context of a broad paradigm that overall responsibility and authority for developing and dispatching communications during an incident will lie with the CMT Communications team, there are two options for organizing and deploying department-specific team members whose responsibilities are primarily communications-related:

- Option 1: Locate the resource with the CMT to enable full, direct coordination of all communications activities during an incident (this is the model most often used by incident management teams)

- Option 2: Make every effort to ensure that any communications-related actions, whether directed to an external or internal audience, are fully coordinated with the CMT prior to releasing any messages

Notwithstanding the above, the DOC may still create and disseminate incident-related "micro (departmental) communications."

Competencies

The Communications Team typically work in a communications-related role, so are expected to possess the skills and experience necessary to execute this function during an incident.

Position activities

- If embedded with the DOC, coordinates with the CMT to ensure that incident-related speaking points, FAQs and other communications-related guidance materials are developed and distributed to those who need them
- Works with the DOC Leader and Planning Leader to assess the incident and its impacts from the departmental perspective
- Identifies audience groups; develops and send incident-related messages to each group

Attends and participates in DOC IAP meeting

DOC notification, activation & initial Incident Action Plan (IAP)

A DOC must be prepared to activate and begin response and recovery activities at any time. The following guidelines will guide the DOC activation procedure.

DOC notification & activation

The activation procedure begins when the Incident Assessment Team (IAT) becomes aware of an incident and, after discussion, determines that the incident meets the criteria for activating the CMT. When that is the case, the CMT will send an activation alert to all DOC Leaders and members.

Initial DOC IAP development

The CMT IAP will contain broad, general objectives. After receiving and reviewing the CMT IAP, each DOC will then develop the more granular DOC objectives that will further guide the DOC's actions in the recovery process.

The DOC team's first IAP meeting after activation and the results of their assessment must be included in the first IAP the DOC submits to the CMT

Ongoing DOC IAP development

The ongoing IAP process is detailed in the chart below. Prior to the end of each operational period, the DOC leader must provide their specific DOC objectives to their CMT Team Leader. The CMT Team Leader will review the IAP, ask questions, and then develop any additional high-level objectives for the CMT. The CMT Team Leader then delivers the combined objectives to the CMT.

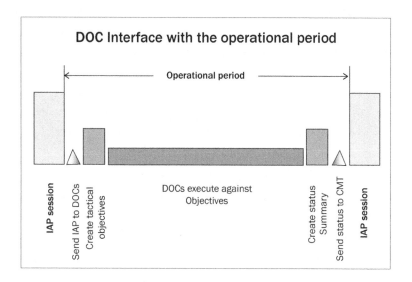

DOC Interface with the operational period

Summary

A Department Operations Center (DOC) can be a great solution for obtaining the most current information from the field as well as communicating out from the CMT. Would it work for your organization? Perhaps – bring together key departments and discuss the concept and explore your options.

CHAPTER 14

Crisis Management plans

Chapter topics
- *Plan benefits*
- *Executive Crisis Management Team and Crisis Management Team plans*
- *Checklist essentials*

❝ Always, always have a plan ❞

— **Rick Riordan**
American author

Introduction

In a fast-moving incident, how often do people pull out their crisis plans at the moment it begins? Actually, not very often. People fall back on their muscle memory[34] and prior experience. That memory is developed through exercises and training over time.

---

34 Muscle memory is not a memory stored in your muscles, of course, but memories stored in your brain that are much like a cache of frequently enacted tasks for your muscles. It's a form of procedural memory that can help you become very good at something through repetition. Source: Life Hacker, May 6, 2011, https://lifehacker.com/5799234/how-muscle-memory-works-and-how-it-affects-your-success

Given that most organizations have few significant events, the experience may be limited. That is not to say that the plans aren't important. Plans include the protocols and procedures that we will follow, the structure that we will fall into and follow, a process for operating, and agreed upon priorities and strategies. That is invaluable. This chapter explores what should be in your crisis management plans.

So, what is the real benefit of a plan?

There's actually a lot of good reasons to spend time developing a quality plan. Let's take a moment to note what some of those are.

1. **Set priorities and direction** – A crisis plan can help to set direction and establish priorities for your response and recovery strategies. It defines your team's view of success and helps to organize team activities. This will help to ensure that the team knows what they should be working on, and what they should be working on first.
2. **Simplify decision-making** – In a crisis, there are lots of things that need to get done. Which is the most important? What do you work on first? Your plan and strategy should have established priorities. Priorities make it easier to stay focused on what is important.
3. **Organize the team** – A pre-identified team structure and organization is critical. When that is known, the team can start moving all in the same direction to achieve the orga-

nization's response and recovery goals.

4. **Align resources for success** – In many crises, there are limited critical resources: people, space, technology, equipment and more. With clear processes, structure and priorities, the team is better equipped for success.

5. **Enable effective communication** – When we all know where you're going and communicate effectively, we have the best opportunity for success. By using our predetermined list of stakeholders, tools, messages and communication strategies, we can maximize your communication success.

Checklists – A Critical Part of any Crisis Plan

When you open any good crisis plan, you should see a position checklist for everyone on the crisis team. Now you may ask, "Why do I need those? After all, the team members are smart and bright people, and everyone knows their job!" Now I am sure that they are indeed smart and bright, but in high stress times, we all need a reminder of what we need to be doing. And your "crisis" job is not your "day" job. There are three basic reasons why checklists are so important:

1. The crisis could be highly stressful (E.g. major earthquake, active shooter) and the team is anxious, overwhelmed and stressed out. Where to start? What to do first or next? A checklist provides a guide.

2. What if they are new to the team? Have had minimal training or no training or exercises? What do they do in

their "crisis job" which is different than their "day job"? A checklist gets them started.

3. While working on the tasks, even though they may be experienced and well-trained, we need to make sure that they did everything they were assigned. A checklist is a great way to review and confrm that you got everything done.

A great book that reinforces these concepts is *The Checklist Manifesto: How to Get Things Right*[35] by Atul Gawande. It demonstrates the value of checklists in fields such as medicine and aviation and makes the case that daily and professional life could benefit from the regular use of checklists. He has done numerous studies that show that checklists create greater efficiency, consistency and safety. Other research has shown that the use of a checklist can save lives, time, money and ensure greater results. But to be effective, they have to be used and followed. What gets in the way of success is not the checklist, but human behavior and the failure to completely follow it. A checklist is critical, but the implementation and its actual use are still a point of weakness.[36]

Plans, plans, plans – Who needs one?

This is a great question and ties directly back to Chapter 5 and the discussion about organizational size and the number of loca-

---

35 The Checklist Manifesto: How to Get Things Right, Atul Gawande, Picador, January 4, 2011

36 Surgical Checklists Save Lives — but Once in a While, They Don't. Why? By Siddhartha Mukherjee, New York Times, May 9, 2018

tions. As discussed in Chapter 5, in smaller organizations (approximately fewer than a thousand employees), you will likely only have one crisis management team that is responsible for both strategic and tactical response activities. Those organizations need one plan.

However, larger organizations should have two crisis management teams and two plans. One team would be comprised of senior executives responsible for strategic activities, and the second one would be a tactical team made up of operational managers who will manage the response and recovery activities. So, most organizations minimally need two plans, maybe more. More on that later.

66 *Just the facts, Ma'am; just the facts.* 99

— **Sergeant Joe Friday**
Dragnet TV show

Plan design

Crisis plans should be action-oriented rather than theory-based. Imagine this: you are standing in a dark parking lot, your building is on fire, you grab your flashlight as you open up your plan. What do you need at that very moment? It should clearly say what you need to do ***right now*** – in simple straightforward language. In a crisis, when a team member opens a plan, it should provide immediate structure, guidance and process – not theory. To that end, all of the plans that we design are structured to be used at the time of crisis. If you want theory, you can read a book like this one!

We believe that the plans should focus on what you need to know right now. The size, structure and organization of plans should reflect that. In other words, give them what they need to be successful in that moment.

Executive Crisis Management Team (ECMT) plan

An executive plan is a high-level overview of roles and re-sponsibilities – plus a bit on process and communication. When I ask executives what they need at time of crisis, this is what I have heard:

- I want to know what others are doing
- I want to know what is expected of me
- I want to know who will contact me, where I should go
- Lastly, I don't want to look stupid or be embarrassed

It makes perfect sense – these individuals lead organizations and people for a living. If you don't tell them their role, they will assume it is to lead the response and recovery – and they will.

Suggested Executive CMT table of contents

So, what should be in the Executive CMT plan? Here is a sug-gested table of contents with some highlights.

- Executive CMT instructions on what to expect

- ○ Communication regarding the crisis from whom, how and when
- ○ Where to meet (physically and virtually)
- Executive CMT Membership, Responsibilities, and Crisis Communication
  - ○ Membership – list all members, contact information and leadership and position succession planning
  - ○ Responsibilities – clearly state their responsibilities
    - Make strategic policy decisions
    - Make strategic financial decisions
    - Act as senior relationship manager for key corporate relationships ranging from employees and their families, government officials, regulatory bodies and strategically important stakeholders and eventually to customers
    - Act as media spokesperson as deemed appropriate and recommended by the Communications executive
  - ○ Crisis Communication – detail who serves as the main spokesperson and source of crisis information for the Executive CMT and what communications the Executive CMT are expected to approve
- Executive CMT Checklists
  - ○ Chair
  - ○ Members
  - ○ Support Team – these individuals document the meeting, provide all logistical support and ensure that the

ECMT has what they need
- Appendix
  - Activity log – forms to keep track of meeting attendance, decisions and action items
  - Document Maintenance and Training – expectations as to how often training and exercises occur and who maintains the plan
  - Glossary

Most of the Executive CMT plans we write are around 13 – 17 pages – short, succinct and to the point. The focus is on responsibilities, communication and reporting.

66 *Planning is bringing the future into the present, so you can do something about it now.* 99

— **Alan Lakein,**
American author

Crisis Management Team (CMT) plan

As we discussed in Chapter 5, there could be several levels of crisis management teams depending on the size and number of locations in your organization. Every team requires a plan – the complexity is driven by the size of the location, the team and what work is performed at that location. The easiest way to understand the plan levels is by using the tier concept we discussed in Chapter 5.

Corporate Crisis Management Team Plan – Tier one

The Corporate CMT is the most complete and complicated of any of your CMTs. It includes the "usual" roles of any CMT such as Facilities, Security, IT and Human Resources, but it also has those departments that are usually only at the Corporate Head-quarters, such as Investor Relations or Legal. It activates to support its own recovery *but* also to support the recovery of *other locations.*

To help make the plans as "action-oriented" as possible, we have divided them into sections. Team members only need the sections (or maybe only pages within a section) that apply directly to them. There are several advantages in organizing the plan this way:

- Flexibility – not everyone needs or wants the whole plan
- Slimmed down plan for the user – they only get what they need
- Avoid "plan overload" which is caused by giving everyone a large document when they actually need very little out of it to do their job
- Ease of maintenance and plan updates - a segmented plan is easier to maintain

So, what does a segmented Crisis Plan look like? Here is an option for you to consider:

- Section 1: Incident Assessment Team (IAT) – the entire assessment process and team. Give to everyone...or just IAT members.
- Section 2: Team Checklists – every team member must

have a checklist. (Most team members need only the part of Section 2 that describes their team and the overall team structure. This could be 5 – 10 pages instead of 75+.)

- Section 3: Reference Materials – how to organize and manage the EOC. (This is usually just for the EOC manager, Business Continuity or Crisis professional managing EOC setup and program maintenance.)

The end result is a greater likelihood that team members will actually read what they need to read. They will be more effective, you will have less wasted paper and maintenance updates will be easier.

Section One: Incident Assessment Team

Section One reviews the three major roles of the Incident Assessment Team (IAT) in detail. Use the steps one through three (noted below) and format them into an easy checklist for the IAT to follow during an assessment call.

Step One: Notify and assess

When any member of the Incident Assessment Team (IAT) becomes aware of a situation that does (or could) become a crisis, s/he will notify other IAT members to review and discuss the known facts and decide on a course of action. There are two possible outcomes to the assessment discussion: "activate" or "don't activate." There is no middle ground.

- **Notify:** When any member of the Incident Assessment Team (IAT) becomes aware of a situation that does (or could) require the attention of the CCMT, he/she will call the <<who??>>, who will notify the Incident Assessment Team (IAT) using the emergency notification system. Who is the who? In many organizations this could be a 24-hour Security Operations Center (SOC) or a Network Operations Center (NOC). You should avoid having an individual person be the contact person as it could lead to a single-point-of-failure if for some reason that person was not available at the moment of the crisis.

- **Assess:** The team assembles virtually – or physically – and assesses the incident using the activation criteria and then makes the decision to activate or not.
  - If **YES,** activate the CCMT: Proceed to Step Two.
  - If **NO**, do NOT activate the CCMT:
    - Document the team's decision and return to "business as usual."
    - Continue to monitor the situation. In this case, establish a time to meet again and re-evaluate the known facts. Continue to periodically assess the situation until a final decision is made.

Step Two: Activate and notify

- **Activate:** If the decision is made to activate:
  - Determine which physical Emergency Operation Center (EOC) to use and activate it
  - Activate the virtual Emergency Operation Center (EOC) as well
- **Notify:**

○ All CCMT members that an activation has been ini-
tiated, using best available communications channels
○ Notify Executive CMT of the activation

Step Three: Plan, brief and assess

- **Plan:** The Incident Commander[37] conducts the first Incident Action Plan (IAP) meeting (Chapter 12) and the
CCMT begins executing assigned response tasks
- **Brief:** Brief the ECMT, the full CCMT, and others as
required
- **Assess:** At the end of the operational period, reconvene
and assess status, new information, and new objectives -
this is the completion of the "full cycle" as noted in Chapter 12 with the Planning P

Repeat: Step Three ("plan, brief, assess") – as long as necessary until the team "stands down."

Section Two: Team checklists

This section deals with the team structure (ICS or not), team
roles and responsibilities and the checklists for each of the team
positions. A typical list of categories in Section 2 includes:

- Roles and Responsibilities of the Corporate CMT
  ○ A high-level review of
    ■ Team structure – the different teams
    ■ Roles and responsibilities of each team

---

37   Individual in charge of the CCMT

*66 In all planning you make a list
and you set priorities. 99*

— **Alan Lakein,**
American author

- Corporate CMT Authority
  - ○ This should clearly state that the CCMT is authorized to activate and mobilize all company resources required to manage a crisis and maintain business operations, integrity, and reputation; the Executive Management Team must designate this authority
- Corporate CMT Structure
  - ○ This discusses the team structure, reporting relationships and how the CCMT fits into the entire crisis reporting structure – who reports to them and to whom they report
- Position Checklist organized by Team
  - ○ Each team position must have a position checklist, which should include:
    - Roles and Responsibilities
    - Activation Actions
    - Operational Actions
    - Deactivation Actions

The following is an example of a sample checklist for the In-cicident Commander (leader of the CCMT).

INCIDENT COMMANDER CHECKLIST

Role
- Lead and coordinate the response and recovery effort

Responsibilities
Specific responsibilities include, but are not limited to, the following:
- Set response and recovery priorities and objectives through the Incident Action Plan (IAP) process
- Direct the acquisition and allocation of all response and recovery resources
- Resolve conflicts within the CCMT
- Implement business policy decisions
- Ensure the timely recovery of time-sensitive business processes

Activation phase actions
- Proceed to the physical or virtual Emergency Operations Center (EOC), or both, as indicated by notification
- Initiate an EOC conference-bridge if unable to be physically present or connect to the virtual EOC
- Obtain most current situation status updates from whatever sources are available
- Take immediate actions necessary to ensure the health and safety of employees, visitors, and the public
- If CCMT Team Leaders have not reported, activate the named alternates to fill critical team vacancies
- Mobilize additional personnel as required to support the initial activation
- Within the first hour of activating, hold the first IAP meeting (reference CCMT Plan Section One)
- Communicate:
    - Initiate Emergency Notification System notifications, as necessary
    - Work with CCMT Executive Liaison to ensure that the Executive CMT is briefed immediately at time of activation and a detailed briefing after the first IAP meeting

CHECKLIST continued on next page

CHECKLIST *CONTNUED*

- If appropriate to the situation, work with the Business Operations Team Leader to direct execution of any affected departments' Business Continuity Plans
- Work with the Communications Leader to ensure that appropriate messages are being developed and dispatched to identified internal and external stakeholders
- Ensure that all Team Leaders have completed and posted their staffing charts (reference CCMT Plan Part Three)
- Review the potential of the incident to become a sustained operation (i.e. extending 24+ hours); in 24+ hour activations, ensure that all staffing plans accommodate alternate shift staffing
- Consider how the situation could escalate and direct any *immediate* actions necessary to isolate and contain the scope of the incident

Operational phase actions
- Oversee preparation of the IAP:
  - Schedule and conduct IAP sessions
  - Establish the Operational Period (i.e. the time of the next IAP session)
- Establish objectives based on current status reports and the Operational Period
  - Direct the preparation of the IAP summary document
  - Review, approve, and authorize distribution of the IAP once it has been prepared
- Maintain full awareness of the overall crisis situation
- Review all external communications for accuracy
- Work with the EOC Manager to establish and communicate recurring briefing schedules (e.g. with Executive Committee and other key stakeholder groups)
- Monitor stress levels in the EOC – pace yourself and other team members.

Brief your back-up CCMT member at shift changes

CHECKLIST continued on next page

CHECKLIST *CONTNUED*

Deactivation phase actions

- Direct the termination of response and recovery activities and the deactivation of the CCMT when the response and recovery effort is completed
- Develop and publish final incident communication(s) to all applicable stakeholders
- Conduct a CCMT after-action debriefing that reviews all aspects of the incident and the response and recovery effort
- Fully document any recommended changes to policies, procedures, equipment, and any other aspect of the effort that may be identified
- Direct the preparation of an After-action Report (reference CCMT Plan Part Three)
- As appropriate, ensure that CCMT employees goes to critical stress debriefings

---

Section Three: Reference materials

This section is primarily used by the EOC Manager and Business Continuity and Crisis Management professionals tasked with managing the physical and virtual EOCs. The following sections are designed to provide good guidance for setting up and managing the EOC (physical or virtual).

- **Appendix A**: Glossary – common terms to ensure we are all talking the same language
- **Appendix B**: Emergency Operations Center (EOC)
  - **EOC Set-Up Checklist** – show how the physical room

should be setup - ideally each team should have their own table

- ○ EOC Team Supplies – list everything you need to run the command center and boxes of supplies for each team
- ○ EOC Room diagram – draw the physical layout of the room
- ○ Communication Within the Emergency Operations Center – explain how communications occur between the Leader and the teams and between the teams
- ○ EOC Status Boards – list the general EOC status boards (this could include static facts, decisions, announcements, regional status) and provide a suggestion list of what should be on each team's status boards
- ○ Sustained Event Considerations – develop a list of suggestions on managing a sustained activation (see Chapter 15)

- **Appendix C:** Virtual Emergency Operations Center (VEOC) – see Chapter 8

- **Appendix D:** Call and Meeting Management – include a step-by-step checklist on how to run an effective call or meeting
  - ○ Initial Incident Assessment Team (IAT) Call or Meeting (sample below)
  - ○ Initial Incident Action Plan (IAP) Call or Meeting
  - ○ Subsequent Incident Action Plan (IAP) Call or Meeting

INITIAL INCIDENT ASSESSMENT TEAM (IAT) CALL / MEETING

1. EOC Manager takes roll as the call begins to document attendance
2. Incident Commander makes opening remarks
3. The individual(s) with the most situational awareness of the incident reviews the incident status information with the participants
4. At the conclusion of the status presentation, the EOC Manager asks for questions from the audience:
   - Does anyone have questions?
   - Do we need any additional information or subject matter expertise (SME)? If so, who? If necessary, get additional SMEs as required
5. The team then discusses the situation
6. At the conclusion of the discussion, the EOC Manager reviews each of the activation criteria:
   - <<list here or reference where criteria can be found>>
7. At the conclusion of the review of the activation criteria, the EOC Manager, "calls the question" to determine if the team should activate; literally speak the question out loud, "Do we activate?"
   - If **YES,** activate the Crisis Management Team:
     - Proceed to Step Two
   - If **NO,** do NOT activate the Crisis Management Team:
     - Document the team's decision and return to "business as usual"
   - **If further monitoring is needed:**
     - Continue to monitor the situation - in this case, establish a time to meet again and re-evaluate the known facts
     - Continue to periodically assess the situation until a "yes" or "no" activation decision has been made
8. Conclude the call, noting next steps

Appendix E: Sample Incident Action Plans (IAP) – include a sample of an IAP to help to visualize what you want in a good IAP.

SAMPLE IAP

March 13, 2018 5:00 AM PT

Situation Status
- A suspicious fire started on the Executive floor (4th floor) at 2:00 AM. The fire alarm sounded and when security officers appeared on the floor, the floor was blanketed in heavy smoke. The fire department arrived at 2:07 AM and began firefighting operations. With no fire sprinklers in the building, the fire spread rapidly, engulfing the entire floor within minutes. The blaze was extinguished at 2:42 AM. Fire investigators are on site. There is no building entry until the investigation is completed. Water from firefighting operations has run down walls and staircases into floors 1 and 2. There were no employee injuries. One fire fighter was treated for smoke inhalation.

Objectives
- Operations (Corporate Infrastructure)
  - Secure building with outside security officers
  - Work with emergency responders (fire, police and ATF)
  - Contact contractors and have on standby to enter facility to conduct an initial damage inspection as soon as building is released to the company
  - Activate company back up locations and prepare for the arrival of designated business recovery personnel
- Technology
  - Activate disaster recovery plan to recover critical infrastructure for the arrival of designated business recovery personnel
  - Transfer main phone numbers to alternate site

SAMPLE IAP continued on next page

SAMPLE IAP *CONTNUED*

- ○ Assess number of additional laptop computers that may be necessary to support critical business processes
- Communications
  - ○ Validate known facts and prepare main talking points for approval
  - ○ Use approved talking points to develop all communications to all stakeholders as noted in the Crisis Communications plan
  - ○ Update company website
- Human Resources
  - ○ Account for all staff using ENS
  - ○ Activate employee assistance program services for any employees who might need them
  - ○ Update the employee hotline with current status
  - ○ Activate the benefits team to answer employee questions regarding pay and benefits
- Planning (Business Operations)
  - ○ Assess RTOs and activate business continuity plans as necessary
  - ○ Determine business impacts and report to the Command team
  - ○ Inventory recovery teams to ensure that they have what they need to conduct business processes
- Finance
  - ○ Notify insurance carriers
  - ○ Set up a disaster accounting code and inform teams

Operational Period - four hours ending @ 9:00 AM PT

Local Crisis Management Team plan – Tier two

The detail and information from the CCMT plan should be used to build all Tier Two Local CMT plans, however the content may have the following likely differences:

- **Section One** – include clear communication requirements and protocols between the Local CMT and the Corporate CMT. In particular the criteria for activation should include language about "impacts to other company locations" or "impacts to business processes." This language is critical to ensure that any IAT thinks beyond themselves and their location and asks the question, "could this impact others?"
- **Section Two** – there are likely fewer checklists because the corporate functions are not represented
- **Section Three** – no differences

Crisis Management Team plan – Tier three

Plans for small locations are usually just a few pages and detail what their smaller crisis team should do. The focus is on safety assessment and communication. A small crisis management team usually has four key roles at time of crisis:

1. Life Safety. Ensure that all employees and visitors are safe and located.
2. Work with emergency responders. If the incident has engaged local emergency responders (police, fire, EMS, others), the crisis team must work with them to both assist them and get information.

3. As soon as possible, conduct an initial assessment. This can be a physical damage assessment and a business operation assessment by reviewing the RTOs and the business continuity plans.

4. Notify the "mothership" (the Local CMT or whomever the team reports up to). This call is to both notify and likely ask for assistance.

Summary

Solid crisis management plans provide a roadmap for how to manage the situation, communicate and recover. Once your plans are developed, use them in all workshop trainings and exercises. The plan improvement process is iterative in nature – like a fine cheese or wine, the plans will improve over time.

CHAPTER 15

Sustained operations and your Emergency Operations Center

Chapter topics
- *Employee safety and health tips*
- *EOC facility design ideas*
- *Administrative considerations*

❝ *The secret of crisis management is not good vs. bad, it's preventing the bad from getting worse* **❞**

— **Margaret J. Wheatley**
American writer and
management consultant

Introduction

Many organizations have not had to activate their Emergency Operations Centers (EOC) for a protracted period of time. The concept of sustained operations is one with which all EOC managers should be familiar in order to maximize their team's performance and minimize the stumbling blocks associated with a prolonged event.

This chapter focuses on three main areas: People, Facilities and Administrative. These activities ideally should be done in advance, however, many could be enacted "on-the-fly" if you experience a protracted activation before you get a chance to implement these actions.

Sustained operations

How do you define sustained operations? Many consider an incident that requires the activation of the Crisis Management Team and the Emergency Operations Center for over 24 hours a sustained event. It is a prolonged working period combined with demanding situations of urgency that can lead to poor performance. The urgency of the situation, the stress of the activation and the extended and excessive hours in sometimes poor conditions can lead to a host of issues including decreased productivity and poor work results.

City, County and Federal teams as well as the military have a lot of experience in this area. Companies and organizations, not so much. It is critical to keep the principals of this chapter in mind during any activation. If you don't care for your team, pretty soon you won't have one. Folks will peel off the team with serious fatigue and illness and may not come back. They can also develop post-traumatic stress disorder (PTSD) from the experience.

People

This list is not in a particular order. Explore each item on this list and see which ones could really help your team maintain their performance, sanity and health.

Nutrition

Ask anybody about their experience of working in an EOC for an extended period of time and one of the first things they will mention is how good or bad the food was. Really. Good food is critical...people working long hours look forward to meal breaks to break up the shift.

When selecting foods for the EOC, consider the following recommendations.

- Minimize sugars and caffeine – The sugar creates a yo-yo blood sugar and causes more fatigue. Excessive caffeine can result in sleep problems.
- Mix complex and simple carbohydrates – Always serve complex carbohydrates along with simple ones (i.e. whole wheat muffin with fruit). This helps to keep blood sugars more even.
- Choose lower fat meals – Low fat meals are easier to digest, people feel less sluggish and tired.
- Avoid really heavy meals – causes more fatigue and sluggishness.
- Grazing is a far better way to eat, small meals every 2-3 hours.
- Discourage alcohol on off-hours; it interferes with deep sleep, often causing the person to waken after only a few hours of sleep, unable to sleep soundly after that.

- Have lots of healthy food choices: fruit, veggies, whole wheat, low fat and less sugar.
- Have simple "safe" food that people can take into the EOC without creating a mess. Food bars or fruit is a great mobile choice. However, discourage eating in EOC overall. People need a break from the place, and the room needs to stay clean.
- Find out if workers have any food allergies or preferences such as vegetarian, lactose intolerant or gluten free.
- Secure a *very good* caterer, always have a backup. This is especially important in the event of a regional disaster such as an earthquake or hurricane.

One of the things that people look forward to is meal times – it gives them a good physical and mental break. Make them good and healthy!

Mental health

Consider having an Employee Assistance Program (EAP) counselor assigned to a shift – maybe not every shift or every day but frequently. Ideally, they would enter the EOC midway through a shift and walk around and observe and talk with people, taking a mental health temperature of the group. They will become aware of problems often before they are obvious to others, and they have the training to help the group or individual deal with it. If you don't use an EAP person for this role, have someone perform this function – possibly the safety officer.

Don't allow problems to escalate. Resolve issues quickly (between workers, teams, etc.) Teams will often be working together in tight quarters, often in stressful conditions and possibly during a seasonally difficult time of the year. Be aware of this and conduct training to help people recognize signs of stress in themselves and others and what to do about it.

Once the initial excitement wears off and it becomes routine, watch for signs of complacency. This is when mistakes tend to happen. When boredom sets in, review procedures with the team to re-engage them in the process. Maybe do some job rotation or reassign to other tasks.

Neck and shoulder massage

In order to ease stress and make workers more comfortable, head and neck massage therapists are a regular practice in many EOC's. A 10-minute neck and shoulder massage can often relieve headaches, reduce stress and allow employees to stay on the job.

Childcare, Eldercare, Petcare

What do you do when mission-critical employees can't come to work due to lack of childcare or eldercare, closed schools or no one to walk their dog? You might first think this is their problem, not yours. Think again – if that team member can't come in, it quickly becomes your problem. Be prepared for this situation. Look into resources in your area for childcare, eldercare and petcare. Think outside the box and look for creative solutions.

Family preparedness

If problems occur in your area and your employees have not prepared their families for an emergency, workers will not stay on the job. Encourage home preparedness and emphasize readiness for the emergencies that are pertinent for your area. There are several great resources online that include printed materials, posters and lesson plans. Two excellent preparedness websites include:

- FEMA – www.ready.gov
- American Red Cross – www.redcross.org

Consider sponsoring employee safety and preparedness fairs and encourage local agencies and vendors to attend making it easy for employees to get information, buy kits and prepare their families. September is national preparedness month – create a great annual program and build on it each year. Check out www.ready.gov/september.

Shift rotation

Most "shift work" experts suggest it is better to stay on one shift rather than rotate shifts, giving the body time to adjust. An ideal schedule is 3 days on, 2 off with 12-hour shifts. Police and Fire Departments commonly use this strategy. It is possible to work more than 3 days in a row if the job is less physical and there are less "life and death" stressful decisions being made.

Transportation

If working 12-hour shifts, consider providing transportation support for workers. Driving when fatigued may result in accidents. Options might be using a shuttle van with drivers for transport or a local transport company. There have been lawsuits in several states when a worker left the job after long hours, fell asleep at the wheel and was killed.

Housing

Working 12-hour shifts results in little time for rest, sleep and relaxation. If workers are housed, fed and their personal issues are minimized, they will be able to do a better job with an aggressive schedule. Consider using a hotel that is close to the EOC for housing. Rooms could be shared with one worker sleeping, then housekeeping cleans, second worker sleeps, the room is cleaned and so on. Or if families are concerned about not seeing their working spouse, assign rooms to families. Although this will probably not result in more rest for the worker, it will likely result in more family peace.

Incentives

Do you provide incentives for those who will have to work during an EOC activation? How will you motivate workers? Incentives may include money, more time off and/or acknowledgement from management.

Communication - EOC briefings

Regular briefings given to the entire EOC will help everyone know what is going on. These should be short, concise, to the point, lasting no more than 5 – 10 minutes. The frequency of these short briefings depends on what is going on – at least every eight hours. These can help to keep everyone involved, ensure that they understand what the key issues are, brings the group together, reduces rumors and further builds the team.

Health

The health of the workers is very important. Encourage flu vaccinations for the entire CMT. Consider having a medical provider come to an EOC meeting and provide free vaccinations. If someone gets sick with a cold or the flu, send them home. One person can make everyone sick. Place hand sanitizers in many locations in the EOC and encourage their use along with good handwashing. Encourage employees to stay well-hydrated, with good nutrition, and frequent rest breaks to combat illness and reduce stress.

Stress reduction

Stress reduction training and techniques are always helpful. Many EAP's do stress reduction training. Encouraging learning stress reduction techniques such as deep breathing, stretching, meditation and many others will help employees stay calm in a crisis. Give a mini-workshop on stress reduction techniques including exercises and give printed materials for employees to read.

Fitness

If possible, provide opportunities for workers to exercise during off time. Check into nearby health clubs or the hotel your team is using. This would be very helpful for stress reduction. Some EOC's have yoga, stretching or relaxation sessions at the end of a shift.

Family issues

Family preparedness training and education are critical for an employee to do well in an EOC. This includes educating employee's families on shift work and its effects, the importance of event and the importance of their family member participating in this effort. If there were family issues and problems before the EOC activation, they may get exacerbated by the work. Be aware of this and involve EAP when possible.

First aid skills

Make sure that a sufficient number of team members in the EOC have basic first aid skills and CPR training. If transportation is affected or medical response is hampered in any way, the EOC may have to deal with its own medical problems longer than they would normally.

Employee hotlines

Regular updates of your employee hot line will provide a valuable communication tool for all employees. It will help to reduce rumors and keep everyone informed on the organization's status during the EOC activation and emergency.

Facilities
Space

The EOC must be sized to handle the maximum anticipated

CMT that would be called in the event of a major disaster. A minimum of 50 square feet per person is required (80 square feet preferred) including restrooms.

When you are attempting to determine your space requirements, consider the amount of equipment any individual work area may need. Also consider the amount of surface area a worker will need to accommodate laptop/desktop computers, binders, reports and writing space.

Emergency power

If you are in an area with major regional events such as a hurricane or earthquake, you must seriously consider having an emergency electrical generator. It must be large enough to power the EOC and all facilities (HVAC, radios, elevator, computer systems, etc.), and is permanently wired with automatic start and transfer. It should be located so that noise or fumes do not interfere with the EOC and include a self-contained fuel system with a minimum four-day reserve.

Communications

During the crisis the EOC must be able to communicate both internally and externally. Consider these communication capabilities:

- Landline phones
- Mobile phones
- Satellite phones (essential for areas with major regional events such as hurricanes or earthquakes)

- Two-way radios can be helpful. Also consider the smaller hand-held radios that have a smaller reach but can be very helpful in communicating with team members in different rooms
- Internet
- Cable television

Break rooms

It is important to have break room space near the EOC, so employees can take a stretch break, get some food or take a mental rest. If it is close by, they can be retrieved if there is an urgent need but otherwise will get a chance to relax. Periodic rests can help to improve the overall performance of the individuals in the EOC.

Rest areas

A rest area or lounge that employees can go to catch a quick "cat nap" or rest if things are slow can help maintain the energy level. Small lightweight folding cots, floor mats or couches are all good options. This is especially helpful on the night shift or during slow periods.

Noise

Noise in an EOC can grow to be a very significant issue. Sound sources include ringing phones, unnecessary conversations, office equipment and poor acoustics. Loud noise will start to undermine people's abilities to process information, think clearly and begin to erode their mental health. Be aware of sound in the EOC and make physical adjustments to the space in advance. Some things that may help include: fabric dividing partitions to break up a larger room; place busier and louder groups toward the corners of a room rather than in the middle; turn off phone ringers and install a light that blinks when a call is received; if televisions are in the room, turn the sound off and keep machines such as copiers and faxes outside of the EOC.

Once you activate the EOC, assign someone to monitor noise levels and intervene as necessary. Interventions may include asking people to take unnecessary conversations outside, holding briefings or meetings in smaller conference rooms and having sound off on televisions in the EOC. The safety officer would often fill this role and report to the Incident Commander.

Housekeeping

How often do most offices have janitorial services? Most offices only have service once a day. That won't work during an activation. Frequent housekeeping services inside the EOC, restrooms, and break areas are essential. It will more than likely be required every shift and at minimum every 12 hours.

Air quality

Stuffy rooms and poor indoor air quality will produce fatigue, dull minds, headaches and less productive employees. Be aware of the room ventilation. As a contingency, have some standing fans for use in crowded rooms to circulate air. Use only "low fume" white board markers. Don't allow any spraying of aerosols in the

EOC. This would include hairsprays, perfumes, fixatives and room fresheners. You may also want to consider a ban on perfumes and colognes as they disagree with so many people, especially in tight quarters.

Lighting

Eye fatigue can lead to headaches, poor performance and fatigue. Soft overhead lighting, indirect lighting sources and natural light will reduce eye fatigue and tend to make workers more comfortable. Avoid placing computers near windows to avoid glare on the screen or the eyes from having to accommodate window light. Consider glare screens if glare is a problem. Share simple exercises to minimize eye fatigue:

- Stare at a fixed object at least 50 feet away for 10 seconds every 30 minutes to cause muscles to refocus
- Cup eyes in palms of hands and rest head in hands for 60 seconds; a great stress reducer

Ergonomics

Folding chairs and six-foot tables may work well in an exercise but are not adequate for a sustained activation. Poor ergonomics will result in worker fatigue, discomfort, pain and the inability to work longer shifts that may be required. A well-designed ergonomic chair with adjustable height, tilt, lumbar support and arms will allow workers to be more comfortable. Ideally computer keyboards will be on adjustable surfaces to accommodate many different size workers. If using laptops, use a "regular mouse" to avoid wrist strain and remember to have mouse pads. Non-glare screens are ideal to minimize eye fatigue. Phone headsets are essential for workers making or receiving frequent calls in order to ease neck and shoulder discomfort.

Non-spill cups only

To avoid the disastrous consequences of a beverage pouring into a laptop, consider instituting a "non-spill cup only" rule. Travel coffee cups (with a spill-proof lid) or bottles of water with a sealing lid will help to prevent a major spill. Some EOC's provide non-spill or "commuter" cups with the organizations logo to promote the practice.

Food rules – To eat or not to eat?

Food in the EOC results is smells, odors, crumbs and other unpleasantness. In order to minimize food issues such as greasy keyboards and rodent concerns, it is highly recommended to institute a no-eating rule in the EOC. If you allow any food in the area, it should be "safe food" such as food bars or fruit.

First aid supplies

Review your hazard risk analysis to ensure that the medical supplies that you have in your first aid kits fit the emergencies you are likely to face in your area. For example, in an earthquake area, the medical supplies should include major dressings and supplies to treat bleeding, cuts, lacerations and other significant injuries. You might want to include non-prescription medications such as aspirin, non-aspirin, ibuprofen, cough medication, vitamin C, cold medication and cough drops for keeping the employees healthy and on the job.

Basic office supplies

Do you have enough of everything you will likely need for at least the first three days? Depending on your location's risk assessment, you may want to have enough for ten days in case there are problems in getting deliveries. This includes all types of office supplies and any items your team will specifically need. This list might include toner, copy paper, markers, flip charts, masking tape, pens, staplers, paper clips and post-it-notes.

Parking

If workers are driving to the EOC, provide secured parking.

Personnel safety

Security is an important consideration in the EOC. All EOC members should have a special EOC badge and there should be badge access only into the EOC. Post Security employees at the main entrance to ensure that no one other than approved employees enter the EOC. Monitor news regarding any reports of civil unrest and act accordingly to ensure employees safety.

Administrative issues
Cash on hand

In regional disasters such as a hurricane or earthquake, cash is king! Vendors will often not take checks, emergency purchase orders or credit cards. Cash may be necessary to purchase basic supplies, equipment and food or to give as an advance to employees. Should you have some cash on hand? How much? How do you safeguard it? Where should it be kept? This should be included in the planning of the Finance team in the EOC.

Emergency purchase orders

Who has authority to prepare emergency purchase orders? This becomes even more challenging if your systems are down. Ask the Finance team to develop a manual process for emergency purchase orders. It should be well documented, step-by-step including all forms that are necessary.

Vendors

Do you have your critical vendors' contact information for weekends, after hours or a holiday in case you need service or supplies? Do you have another company who can act as a backup (phones, office equipment, computers etc.)? Are some of your key vendors already obligated to other customers in a major incident and may not be available or might drain all of their resources? An example might be your cafeteria vendor may also have contracts with hospitals and primary responders who are contracted to get the service first. Ask questions and document responses and solutions in the Finance plan.

Safety

Always consider safety in the EOC. A command center often has many small hazards that have the potential to turn into big accidents. Blocked fire exits, dangling cords, employees standing on office chairs and trip hazards are just some of the common dangers.

An EOC Safety Officer is a person with the authority and responsibility to find the safety hazards and then correct them to avoid accidents. This is a required position in public EOCs and the position resides in the Command Team. This is a critically important job – often in the midst of the crisis, safety is not considered. This results in people being injured, poor morale and inadequate staffing.

Summary

Sustained operations require careful planning to ensure the best results. Much of this planning must be done in advance to ensure success. Engage the Crisis Management Team in the conversation, find out their needs and develop your plan accordingly. Your people are your number one asset – make plans to ensure their success.

FOUR

Program reassessment and reflection

66Without reflection,
we go blindly on our way,
creating more unintended consequences,
and failing to achieve anything useful.99

— **Margaret J. Wheatley**
American writer and
management consultant

You have done a lot of work to get to this point. But in some ways, you have only just begun. Now that you have a program, a team and plans in place, how do you ensure that it is "always on" and is ready at a moment's notice? There are the twists and turns in any program – team member turnover as well as the need to keep challenging those who have been doing the work for some time.

One of the things that will set your crisis management program apart from others is a commitment to annual reassessment, reflection and updating. You will need to find new ways to keep it fresh in the minds of the members, deepen their learning and expand their skills as the threat universe continues to multiply and evolve. One of the best ways, of course, is creating more engaging and challenging exercises to develop reflexes and muscle memory.

You have come this far – you want to make sure that the program continues to mature and develop over time. To make this happen, this final section may be the most important to the long-term health of your program.

CHAPTER 16

Continual improvement –
Crisis Management Team
and program development

Chapter topics
- *The importance of regular exercises*
- *Ideas for team engagement*
- *Executive sponsor involvement*
- *Use your governance plan*
- *After incident follow-up*

66 *A sense of humor is part of
the art of leadership,
of getting along with people,
of getting things done.* **99**

— **Dwight D. Eisenhower**
36th President of the United States

Introduction

Now that you've built the program, team, and plans, how do you keep everyone ready?

Your Crisis Management Team must be prepared for all types of events because there is, of course, no way to predict what you will face. As we've discussed, crises could range from physical catastrophes to a cyberattack. The added challenge is that almost every crisis has twists you might not have encountered before or anticipated. That means that you have to be able to spot the unexpected and quickly adapt.

To deal with unanticipated challenges, your team has to be:

1.   In a constant state of readiness – as near to instantaneous as possible
2.   Ready for a wide-range of contingencies

How do you ready your team for that? You need to find new and innovative ways to keep them engaged, learning and ready for anything.

Exercises – the closest thing to real you can get

I am a big proponent of exercises. Exercises are your best way to deepen your team members' knowledge, develop their skills, change their behaviors, and test their responses. I also believe that exercises provide you with a golden opportunity to validate and promote your plan and, importantly, engage senior management.

Exercises are a civilian form of military war games. They test strategies and responses without anyone getting hurt. An exercise scenario – the story -- has the power to deeply engage the exercise players by dropping them into close to real-world situations. In the exercise, your team must make tough decisions under realistic pressure, develop action-plans and execute critical responses. Reading a plan or sitting around discussing things in a conference room will never do that.

If you've never staged a serious exercise, I strongly suggest that you lay the groundwork for one. It will open the eyes of executives and colleagues to the real challenges of dealing with real crises. Spend the time to develop a quality experience that continues to expand their understanding, deepen their knowledge and refine their skills. As we discussed in Chapter Ten, you need to move your team into more challenging exercises to truly deepen their knowledge.

I jokingly call a basic tabletop exercise a "blah-blah-blah" exercise because people simply say what they "would do" to solve a problem given to them. There is no push back, no difficulties or responses such as "we tried that, and it didn't work." To really get someone into the situation, it has to be fully simulated with "simulation teams" (think of them as the "enemy" in a war game). The simulation team – always in a different room – reveals new facts about the changing situation as the exercise unfolds. Those so-called "injects" can range from information from emergency responders to videos of local news media reports. I've never seen a crisis team that didn't learn from and greatly value such an exercise. (My first book, *Emergency Management Exercises – From Response to Recovery*, details how to develop these more engaging exercises.)

Annual exercise and training calendar

Do you have an exercise or training calendar in your organization? If you are like most, the answer is likely "no." Do you want to raise the bar for your team? Then develop a *multi-year training and exercise plan*.[38] This is a foundational document for guiding a successful crisis management exercise program. One of the key aspects of this document is that it ties training and exercise activities to the organization's crisis management and business continuity management (BCM) goals. A great idea! It utilizes a building block approach for training and exercise activities and demonstrates how training and exercise activities support the identified BCM priorities.

As training and exercises are completed, the document can be updated annually (at a minimum) or modified to reflect changes to the priorities and new capabilities that need to be assessed. When starting to craft your program, there are two main underlying themes to remember:

1.   Think in terms of a building block approach
2.   Tie activities to the program goals

Effective team development is based on a series of building blocks, starting with providing training and workshops (often combined with Orientation exercises) and then continuing to challenge the team until they have reached their appropriate competency level.

Once you have established the basic skill set, your bi-annual

---

38   Emergency Management Exercises – From Response to Recovery, Regina Phelps, Chandi Media, December 2010

exercise activity becomes a deepening of the skills at that exercise-type level. This logical progression of exercises helps to build capabilities and competence.

When starting out conducting exercises, begin with an *Orientation* exercise and work your way "up" (in complexity) from there. Many organizations will reach their appropriate competency level at a *Tabletop* exercise while some will advance to a *Functional* exercise. With the exception of public-sector entities, the overly ambitious, or those with field response requirements, few organizations advance to a *Full-scale* exercise. For the definitions of all of these types of exercises, check the Glossary.

Tie exercise activities to program goals

Do you have goals for your BCM program? Are those goals for one year? Multiple years? What would it look like if you plotted those goals out over time and tied the goals to training and exercises for the appropriate teams? This document could be reviewed and approved by the BCM Steering Committee and used to measure performance annually while demonstrating another way that your program provides value.

Team member engagement

Employees join the crisis management team but, since there are likely very few activations, how do they remember what their job is, where they meet and how they deal with a host of other issues? Or maybe they just got an email from their boss appointing them to this new team and they wonder, what am I supposed to do?

How do you keep team members engaged and understanding their roles and responsibilities? Here are a few tips.

Keep everyone in the loop

Periodic emails, mini-newsletters, webinars, team calls, tips and reminders sent through your emergency notification system are just some of the ways to remind and educate team members about their role. The list is endless. Think about your organization's culture and what would work to provide members with mini-training sessions, quick reminders or tips about their role. You can also use real-time issues in the organization or the news media as a great training opportunity.

So how might this work? Let's say a well-known brand name company experiences a major incident that turns into a brand and reputational nightmare. While this story is still in the news, use it as a training opportunity to explore how you would have handled it. Start from the very beginning: How would it have come to your Incident Assessment Team's attention? What would their response be? How would communications be handled, what would you say to whom and when? Take the real-life issues as they happen and use them as a training tool – "what if this happened to us?"

Onboarding new members

There is often a fair amount of turnover in a team among the primary and backup members. How do you bring new members into the group and give them the skills they need to be successful?

First, you need to have an orientation plan and a well-crafted slide deck to provide a solid overview. Remember when people are learning something new for the first time – they are trying to see how they fit in, what they are supposed to do and how it all works. Make the training materials easy to understand and visually attractive.

Schedule 30 – 60 minutes to review the materials – with a special emphasis on role and responsibility, how the entire process works, and in particular, how it starts and how they are notified. If they don't know the key leadership of the CMT, include a quick meet-and-greet session with those leaders so the new member will feel welcome.

Some of the terms and language of the crisis management program may be unknown to the new member, so make a simple card that has the terms and abbreviations and quick definitions, so they can follow along and not get lost in the first few minutes. The acronyms in particular can make a newcomer's head spin when they first start.

Lastly, check back with them a few weeks after your training to see if they have any questions or need any clarifications.

Ripped from the news

Another great way to build muscle memory is what we call "Ripped from the News Exercises." These are short exercises to practice a particular skill such as incident assessment or developing an incident action plan. They are super simple and fun to do. You can do one at a CMT meeting (face-to-face or virtual) or some occasion when your team (or part of it) comes together. All you do is open a newspaper and find an appropriate story that fits your organization's risk profile (fire, flood, shooting, fiber cut, cyber breach). Read it carefully, then spend a few moments framing it to your organization, and begin. It's very easy and very effective.

Executive sponsors – Keeping them involved

Ongoing education

Periodic short and timely communications from you about the program are a great way to keep Executive Sponsors aware of risks, current strategies and opportunities for improvement. Here are a few examples. When a major crisis occurs in a well-known company, it's a great opportunity to speak with your Sponsor about how that type of incident would be managed through the crisis management process in your organization. Analyze it from the moment it occurs, how it is brought into the assessment process, and how the teams would respond. If you think you have areas of concern or holes in the process, bring those up and discuss solutions.

Tip: Set up "Google Alerts" to follow industries like yours and your risk profile and see what is delivered to you from Google every day. Let's say you are a manufacturer of widgets and you operate in five countries with the following risks: earthquake, flooding, high winds, terrorism and fire. Enter into your Google Alert Search: Widget Manufacturer, earthquake, flooding, high winds, terrorism, fire, <<list the five countries>>

Then every day, Google will send you anything that matches

your search. Occasionally you will get a story about a competitor or something going on in that region that you didn't know about. Do a bit more research on the link so you can be sure it is a solid piece of news and then forward that to your Sponsor. They likely haven't heard about it either. That kind of communication educates them about the risks, what is happening in those areas, how your program would respond and what else needs to be done to improve overall resiliency. Not inconsequently, it will show them you are on top of what's going on in crisis management.

Carry the torch for Crisis Management and Business Continuity CM/BC

Periodically throughout the course of the year, you will want your Sponsor to "carry the torch" for the CM program, e.g., at budgeting time, when you're staging an exercise, etc. Your sponsor can make the difference between being minimized and under-funded and being seen as a strategic imperative. How do you do that? Here is a short list to get you started. Have your Sponsor:

- **Kick off your bi-annual exercises** – by thanking everyone for participating and emphasizing the critical importance of this work.
- **Brief senior management** peers and the board periodically – so they recognize the risks of underfunding the function and the value of exceptional readiness.
- **Acknowledge crisis team members** – for working hard in an activity that is over and above their "daytime job." (This is particularly important after a CMT activation. In

that case, a letter of appreciation to each team member from the Sponsor and/or the CEO, with copies to their manager and into their personnel file. There could also be a public "shout-out" at a company town hall meeting or bringing them into the executive committee meeting so they can be recognized for their crucial work.)

- **Support adding "credit" for CMT duties to members' annual performance evaluations** – because employees can spend many hours doing training, exercises or real activations in addition to core job requirements.

> 66 *By failing to prepare,*
> *you are preparing to fail.* 99
> —**Benjamin Franklin,**
> A founding father of the United States

Use your Governance Plan to drive your program

As we discussed in Chapter Ten, your governance plan will really work to support your program. The governance document should clearly lay out expectations for the program and can be used as a carrot and stick to keep your program on track.

Ideally you have a Crisis Management/Business Continuity

Steering Committee that will really put some teeth into your program. The Steering Committee should work with you to establish the metrics to help drive the program. They then should review exercise findings, after action reports (AAR) from any activations, findings from internal audit and any recommendations regarding Crisis Management/Business Continuity.

Speaking of Internal Audit, that too can be your friend in building and maintaining your program. Share the governance plan with them and, in particular, the metrics that you have created to measure team capabilities. They can use that when they are doing their audits. It is another way to get departments, groups and teams more engaged in the work.

You have a crisis – Great news!

It is an odd profession to be in – you spend lots of time preparing hoping that nothing will happen! When you do have an incident that requires an Incident Assessment Team review and Crisis Management Team activation, it is essential that you prepare an after-action report. The After-Action Report, or AAR, is a formal record of the incident and a complete summary of the experience. The AAR serves several important functions. The AAR is where you will:

- Document response activities
- Identify successes and problems
- Assess plans and programs
- Develop a plan of action

After-action report

The After-Action Report table of contents should contain the following information:

1. Executive summary and principal recommendations
2. Incident overview
   a. Chronology of events
   b. Incident Action Plans (Copies of the actual IAPs of the incident)
   c. Any pertinent Statistics
   d. Any pertinent maps or photos
3. Event staffing
   a. Note all participants
4. Critical incident debriefing notes (what worked and challenges/opportunities for improvement) focusing on four areas:
   a. Strategic
   b. Organizational
   c. Operational
   d Equipment
5. Next steps
   a. Task list
   b. Individual(s) responsible
   c. Estimated completion date

Report follow-up

Once the report is written, edited, and ready to be sent, you may think that you can take a deep breath and relax as you sink into a cozy chair. Not yet! Like everything in the field of crisis management, you are really never done. Here's your short list of what you should be thinking about now:

- Getting the report in front of the right people
- Gaining consensus on a plan of action
- Tracking the after-exercise task list and any follow-up required to ensure completion of all tasks

Getting the report in front of the right people

This is an important step. Acceptance of the report and recommendations by key individuals is likely tied to funding and other key resources. You need to identify the "right people." Here is a partial list to consider:

- Your executive sponsor
- Corporate Risk Committee
- Senior management
- Senior audit management

In many cases, getting the AAR in front of the "right people" is simply a matter of sending it to them. However, getting them to read it requires a little more thought. It is always good to consider what the hook is for them – what speaks to each of them in particular? They may pay more attention to the report if you can tie the recommendations to:

- Financial goals
- Commitments to clients and customers
- Company audit results
- Key company initiatives

- Areas that you know will "strike a chord" with senior management

Do your research and find out each key player's particular interest. Some gentle words of caution: This report might be fraught with peril depending on the contents and could turn into a political quagmire in your organization. Talk with your sponsor and other trusted colleagues before releasing the report. It is always good advice to tread lightly and be observant at all times.

Gain consensus on a plan of action

Now is a great opportunity to actively engage your Crisis Management/Business Continuity Steering Committee. If they aren't meeting in the near future, schedule a call or quick meeting so you do not lose momentum. Brief them on the recommendations and any applicable new standards. Chart a course of action that will result in the successful resolution of the recommendations. As part of this plan, you will need to develop strategies for:

- Plan revisions – what needs to be changed
- Any new assignments – who is doing what
- Revised budget – required funding to achieve the necessary results

Tracking and follow-up

Once you have an agreed upon a new plan of action, take time to chart all recommendations and action steps, including a timeline to complete each. All deliverables need an owner and a completion date; some may also include intermediate dates as "touch points." Don't forget to consider whether you have the resources you need to achieve the recommendations. This includes people, applications, equipment, and other items. If you discover you have a shortfall, determine the possible work-arounds to gain approval.

Summary

You made it. You have developed a program, plans, teams and a solid structure to ensure its success over time! Remember that all of this work is iterative – it improves, grows and morphs over time. Your goal is to keep moving the program forward!

Congratulations!

> 66 *Some people dream of success,*
> *while other people get up every morning*
> *and make it happen.* 99
>
> — **Harry Wayne Huizenga Sr.**
> American entrepreneur
> and businessman

Glossary

- **Activation criteria** – Criteria used to guide the Incident Assessment Team in determining if crisis plans should be activated.

- **After-Action Report (AAR)** – A summary of lessons learned from an exercise or an incident. The AAR also includes recommendations for improvements.

- **Briefing Schedule** – A briefing schedule is developed once an operational period has been established. During this time, briefings are scheduled with the Executive Crisis Management Team, key leaders, customers, the public, the media and other identified key stakeholders. It is updated as the situation dictates.

- **Business Continuity Plans (BCP)** – The documentation of a predetermined set of instructions or procedures that describe how an organization's mission/business functions will be sustained during and after a significant disruption.

- **Business Continuity exercise** – A mechanism to test the recovery of a mission-critical business process or business department.

- **Business Impact Analysis (BIA)** – The study of an enterprise's requirements, processes, and interdependencies used to characterize technology and business unit contingency requirements and priorities in the event of a significant disruption.

- **Corporate Crisis Management Team (CCMT)** – The CCMT is the tactical team of operational managers who will lead the response and recovery activities for the organization.

- **Crisis Communications** – Crisis communications is designed to protect and defend a company, or organization facing a public challenge to its reputation and brand.

- **Crisis Management Team (CMT)** – The tactical team in charge of managing an incident from response through recovery. In an organization with several tiers, this might be the smallest team. In a small organization, the only crisis team would be called the CMT.

- **Cyber attack** – A breach targeting an enterprise's use of cyberspace for the purpose of disrupting, disabling, destroying, or maliciously controlling a computing environment/infrastructure; or destroying the integrity of the data, or stealing controlled information. A term commonly used by the media.

- **Cyber incident** – Actions taken through the use of computer networks that result in an actual or potentially adverse effect on an information system and/or the information residing in that system.

- **Cyber security** – The ability to protect or defend the use of cyberspace from cyber attacks.

- **Department Operations Center (DOC)** – A DOC is a physical facility or location similar to the company's Emergency Operations Center (EOC) and is established and activated by individual departments to coordinate and control actions specific to that department during an incident.

- **Disaster Recovery Exercise (DRE)** – A mechanism to test the technology recovery aspects of a plan.

- **Disaster Recovery Plan (DRP)** – A written plan for recovering one or more information systems at an alternate facility in response to a major hardware or software failure or destruction of facilities.

- **Drill** – A supervised field response activity with a limited focus to test a particular procedure. Drills usually highlight and closely examine a limited portion of the overall emergency response plan.

- **Emergency incident** – An event or occurrence that 1) requires an immediate response to bring the situation under control and restore normality and 2) can threaten the health or safety of those involved, responders, and people in the surrounding area.

- **Emergency management** – The organization and management of resources and responsibilities for dealing with all aspects of emergencies, including mitigation, preparedness, response, and recovery.

- **Emergency Operations Center (EOC)** – An established location/facility at which selected management can receive information pertaining to an incident and from which they can provide direction, coordination, and support to emergency operations.

- **Emergency Operations Center Manager (EOC Manager)** – Responsible for ensuring that the EOC is managed and that processes are maintained. He/she is an integral resource for the Incident Commander in the internal workings and processes of the EOC.

- **Emergency Response exercise** – A mechanism to test the ability of an Incident Management Team to handle a defined event according to the response aspects of a plan.

- **Emergency Response Plan** – An Emergency Response Plan that establishes an organizational structure and procedures for response to life safety emergencies.

- **Executive Crisis Management Team (ECMT)** – The ECMT is comprised of the senior executives, what is often called the "C-Suite." They perform strategic roles at time of disaster including: strategic policy oversight, approval of large expenditures, acting as media spokespersons as requested by the Communications team, and senior relationship managers for identified key stakeholders.

- **Executive Liaison** – An Executive Liaison position provides a bridge between the ECMT and the CCMT and helps to make sure that communication is flowing back and forth, and that decisions and issues are communicated promptly.

- **Executive Sponsor** – An executive sponsor is often a C-level executive who has a vested interest in seeing a project to completion.

- **Exercise Design Team** – A group of individuals who are tasked with assisting in the design of the exercise. These individuals are commonly subject matter experts from the organization. Their role includes validating the exercise narrative and developing the exercise injects.

- **Exercise Facilitator/Director** – The individual in charge of the exercise from design through the delivery of the exercise. He or she may also be the author of the After-Action Report.

- **Exercise injects** – Information that is inserted or "injected" into the in-progress exercise that expands the story, provides information, asks a question, and/or requires the exercise players to "do something."

- **Exercise plan** – A document outlining the complete background of the exercise, including the narrative. The exercise plan provides all of the necessary background information for the players to begin the exercise. Sometimes called the "players' book."

- **Exercise players** – All participants in the exercise who are responsible for responding to the event.

- **Exercise script** – The text of the exercise injects.

- **Exercise team** – The entire team of individuals who are involved in the management of the exercise. This includes the exercise facilitator/director, exercise Design Team, Simulation Team, Evaluator, Controller, and Observers, but not the players.

- **Full-scale exercise** – A mechanism to test the mobilization of all (or as many as possible) of the response components. A full-scale exercise takes place in "real time," employs real equipment, and tests several emergency functions.

- **Functional exercise** – A mechanism to simulate a disaster in the most realistic manner possible *without* moving the people or equipment to a real site. A functional exercise utilizes a carefully designed and scripted scenario with timed messages and communications between simulators and players.

- **Goal** – A broad statement of the reason the exercise is being conducted. The goal explains what is being assessed or evaluated.

- **Governance Document** – The governing document sets out the program objectives or purposes, responsibilities and how the program is to be administered.

- **Hard Incident** – Something you can tangibly see and feel; in other words, an event where there is a physical impact. Fires, earthquakes, floods, tornadoes, hurricanes, mudslides and violence at work are examples of a hard incident.

- **Helicopter View** – A broad sweeping view of the overall organization.

- **Incident** – An occurrence caused by either human action or a natural phenomenon that requires actions to prevent or minimize loss of life, or damage to property and prevent or minimize disruption to business operations.

- **Incident Action Plan (IAP)** – A document that contains situation status, incident objectives reflecting the overall incident strategy and specific tactical actions, assignments and supporting information for the next operational period of an incident.

- **Incident Assessment Team (IAT)** – The team responsible for evaluating incidents, assigning an incident level, and determining if plans should be activated.

- **Incident Commander (IC) -** The **Incident Commander** is the person responsible for all aspects of a crisis response.

- **Incident Command System (ICS)** – A management system designed to enable effective and efficient crisis management. It provides a standardized approach to the command, control, and coordination of a crisis by providing a common hierarchy for facilities, equipment, personnel, procedures, and communications, all operating within a common organizational structure.

- **Incident levels**: A bit of shorthand to quickly describe an incident and its impact. Often shown as levels (1 through 3, or 1 through 5) or colors (red, yellow, green).

- **Joint Information Center (JIC)** – A central location where communications personnel with communication responsibilities perform critical emergency information functions, crisis communications, and public affairs functions.

- **Local Crisis Management Team (LCMT)** – The LCMT is the tactical team of operational managers who will lead the response and recovery activities at the local level. These individuals are responsible for all the recovery activities and implementing the CCMT decisions.

- **Maximum Tolerable Downtime** – The amount of time mission/ business processes can be disrupted without causing significant harm to the organization's mission.

- **Mothership** – The "mothership" is the corporate headquarters.

- **National Incident Management System (NIMS)** – A system mandated by U.S. Homeland Security Presidential Directive 5 that provides a consistent nationwide approach for governments, the private sector, and non-governmental organizations to work effectively and efficiently together to prepare for, respond to, and recover from domestic incidents, regardless of cause, size, or complexity.

- **Objectives** – The specific activities and deliverables that will be required in an exercise.

- **Observers** – Persons who, during an exercise, are assigned to teams or groups specifically to assess the activities that they observe. Their evaluation is made against the exercise objectives. Observers are sometimes referred to as evaluators.

- **OODA loop** – The OODA loop – observe, orient, decide, and act – was developed by Colonel John Boyd during his time teaching at the Weapons School in the 1960s – 1970s.

- **Operational Period** – The period of time scheduled for execution of a given set of operation actions as specified in the Incident Action Plan. Operational Periods can be of various lengths although usually not over 24 hours.

- **Orientation exercise** – A mechanism to test a response team that uses a simple narrative. It is often delivered in a *PowerPoint* slide presentation in a conversational, non-threatening manner. It is often used to orient a team to a plan.

- **"Parking lot"** – A flip chart or whiteboard that will be used to capture any questions or issues that come up during the exercise or training but can't be addressed at that time. The usual practice is to revisit any "parking lot" issues at the end of the allotted time and make a plan for addressing any unresolved questions or issues then.

- **Participant instructions** – Informs the exercise players of what *they* can expect from the exercise and what is expected of *them* during the exercise.

- **Planning P** – The Planning "P" is a picture of all of the stages in the incident action planning process. Developed by the U.S. Coast Guard, it is a great visual tool to teach IAP development.

- **Preparedness** – The wide range of deliberate, critical tasks and activities necessary to build, sustain and improve the operational capability to prevent, protect against, respond to and recover from domestic incidents.

- **Recovery Point Objective (RPO)** – The point in time to which data must be recovered after an outage.

- **Recovery Time Objective (RTO)** – The overall length of time an information system's components can be in a recovery phase before negatively impacting the organization's mission or mission/business functions.

- **Return on Investment (ROI)** – Return on investment or ROI measures how much money or profit is made on an investment as a percentage of the cost of the investment.

- **Remediation** – The act of correcting a vulnerability or eliminating a threat, for example installing a patch, adjusting configuration settings, or uninstalling a software application.

- **Resilience** – The ability to quickly adapt and recover from any known or unknown changes to the environment through holistic implementation of risk management, contingencies and continuity planning.

- **Soft Incident** – Soft incidents are events where there is an impact to an organization's business and potential damage to the brand or reputation with little or no physical damage. Soft incidents are insidious – they usually don't leave behind any physical evidence.

- **Simulation** – The imitation of the operation of a real-world process or system over time. Something that is made to look, feel, or behave like something else especially so that it can be studied or used to train people.

- **Situational Awareness** – The ability to identify, process, and comprehend the critical elements of information regarding an incident.

- **Sustained Operations** – The activation of a Crisis Management Team and the Emergency Operations Center for over 24 hours in a sustained event. It is a prolonged working period combined with demanding situations of urgency that can lead to poor performance.

- **Status Board** – A physical or virtual board (or both) that contains incident information pertinent to the team who owns it.

- **Tabletop exercise, Advanced** – Same as a Basic Tabletop, with the addition of a Simulation Team present in the exercise room.

- **Tabletop exercise, Basic** – A process to test an organization's emergency management plan and procedures and to highlight issues of coordination and assignment of responsibilities. Basic Tabletop exercises use written and verbal scenarios to evaluate the effectiveness of the team. Tabletop exercises do not physically simulate specific events: nor do they utilize equipment or deploy resources.

- **Threat** – Any circumstance or event with the potential to adversely impact organizational operations (including mission, functions or reputation), organizational assets, individuals, other organizations, or the nation through an information system via unauthorized access, destruction, disclosure, modification of information, and/or denial of service.

- **Tier Levels** – Organizing a crisis program based on company size, number of locations and size of the facilities. If there is more than one office, you automatically have a tier system. The headquarters is tier one, and the second office is tier two. The crisis management team at the tier two site likely has fewer individuals and does not have some of the functions that are solely at the corporate headquarters.

- **Value on Investment** – Intangible assets that contribute heavily to an organization's performance.

- **Virtual Emergency Operations Center (VEOC)** – A virtual collaborative command center equipped with many of the tools of a physical EOC.

Made in United States
Orlando, FL
18 April 2022

16956654R00163